The Civil War in Grundy County and Southern Middle Tennessee

By

Michael Clinton Oliver

2018

Dedication

A very special "thank you" to the many people who helped me with this project. I would like to thank my high school history teacher, the late Donnie Ladd, the late Dr. Bart McCash and Dr. Fred Colvin from Middle Tennessee State University; Dr. Toby Williams and Dr. John Chilton from Trevecca Nazarene University. They made history exciting and fun. I would like to thank the famed Vanderbilt Agrarian Andrew Lytle who took me under his wing and treated me like the son he never had and got me started on this writing journey. Also, a special thanks to the late Ralph Thompson, to Ray Winton, Tim and Cardelia Spicer, Larry Hall, Todd Payne, Janice White, Janelle Taylor, Jimmy Haley, and Jackie Partin for their reading and suggestions. To these and the many more people who have helped, I want to say, "Thank you." A special thanks to my wife Melody for her inspiration and support.

This Book is dedicated to Dr. John and Sara Chilton.

Dr. John Chilton was my beloved history teacher at Trevecca University; but he was much more than that. He is the personification of a true Southern Gentleman. He has been a lifelong mentor, friend, and father figure. He is an amazing storyteller, and no one I have ever met comes close to him in his knowledge of history. Dr. Chilton has continued to be one of the greatest teachers I have ever had inside and out of the classroom.

Sara Chilton is the perfect complement to her husband; she is soft-spoken, kind, and without pretention. She has had a major impact on my family. Brilliant in her own right, she has my love and admiration. Thanks for all your help.

Love you, Papa John and Mama Sara.

Michael Clinton Oliver

2018

Author's Note

My grandmother Mary Conn Payne Mayes was born in Grundy County, Tennessee in 1880. I knew her for only a short time, but many memories are still vivid in my mind. The Civil War was very fresh in her mind. She had known men who lost arms and legs, and women who had lost husbands and sons in what she always called the War Between the States or the War of Northern Aggression. She told me stories, many of which I wish I could still recall. One story that stuck permanently in my ten-year old mind was about Calvin Brixey. My grandmother was a stern woman and when I became rowdy, she told me that Calvin Brixey would get me. As my grandmother related stories of Calvin Brixey's deeds, he became synonymous in my mind with the devil. It wasn't until I began this project that I realized that he came close.

Table of Contents

Prelude to War	7
Causes of War	20
Birth of the Confederacy	42
Tennessee	54
Grundy County	63
Farming	87
War	100
1862	109
1863	134
Foraging	169
Bushwhackers	191
Final Campaign	214
Aftermath	241

The Civil War in Grundy County and Southern Middle Tennessee

Prelude to War

The Civil War has been described as the "most important and powerful single event in American history . . . . It was more important, more powerful in shaping the nation than the Revolution itself which gave birth to the nation."[1] Referred to in the South as the War Between the States, the War for Southern Independence, or by some as the War of the Northern Invasion, the war devastated the nation, and especially the South. In terms of lives lost and soldiers maimed and scarred, nothing comparable had been seen up to that time. Brothers often chose different sides and communities were split over the conflict. The resulting physical, mental, and emotional suffering lasted well into the twentieth century.

Cities were looted and burned. Farms were stripped of everything valuable. Immense regions of once fertile land were laid barren. A congressional committee would later calculate

Tennessee's losses at $185 million. This did not include the loss of earning power and labor caused by the loss of men who were killed or wounded in the war. It would take the nation decades to recover, and the consequences of the war impoverished the South for years to come.

But why did the war happen? Less than one hundred years after the colonies banded together to fight for their independence from the British, they were at war with each other. States' rights, sectional differences, opposing economic interests, tariffs, and slavery all provide partial answers. The Southern perspective differs greatly from the Northern viewpoint. The American Revolution left two questions unresolved. In 1776 there were serious concerns as to whether a democratic society could hold itself together in the face of internal struggle. Most long-lasting civilizations up to that point had been some form of a monarchy, and many doubted the ability of a democracy to exist amid dissension and conflict. Abraham Lincoln asked that question in the opening of his most famous speech, the Gettysburg Address: *"Four score and seven years ago our fathers brought forth on this*

---

[1] James McPherson, *Great Minds in History*. (John Wiley and Sons Inc. New York, 1999), 55.

continent, a new nation, conceived in Liberty, and dedicated to the proposition that all men are created equal. Now we are engaged in a great civil war, testing whether that nation, or any nation so conceived and so dedicated, can long endure."[2]

The second question and one of almost equal importance was that of slavery. Could America exist half free and half slave? Despite the words of the Declaration of Independence that "all men were created equal," slavery was woven into the economic, political, and cultural fabric of the South.

Slavery had at one time been entrenched in the North. As industry became more important, slavery had been virtually abolished above the Mason-Dixon Line. In the agrarian South, the invention of the cotton gin had made cotton more valuable and slaves indispensable.

The Civil War would eventually settle both these questions. The union of states could survive in time of crisis. It would endure. The nation could not exist part slave and part free. The Civil War settled that question forever.

The seeds of war sprouted during the middle part of the

---

[2] Abraham Lincoln, Gettysburg, Pennsylvania, November 19, 1863. Italics mine. http://www.abrahamlincolnonline.org/lincoln/speeches/gettysburg.htm.

19th century. Sectional differences became more evident as both sides tried to protect their economic interests. During the first half of the 1800's, abolitionist and pro-slavery supporters fought a war of words that would foreshadow the bloodshed that was to come.

The first state to legalize slavery had been Massachusetts in 1641, and it was directed primarily at the Native American population.[3] Massachusetts' colonists raided a neighboring Pequot village, and those that were captured were sold into slavery in the West Indies or exchanged for African slaves. Massachusetts, like many American colonies, had roots in a scrupulous fundamentalist Protestantism. Christianity was no barrier to slave-ownership, however. The Puritans regarded themselves as God's Elect, and so they had no difficulty with slavery, which had the sanction of the Law of the God of Israel. The Calvinist doctrine of predestination easily supported the Puritans in a position that blacks were a people cursed and condemned by God to serve whites. Cotton Mather said that blacks were the "miserable children of Adam and Noah," for

---

[3] https://ferris.edu/HTMLS/news/jimcrow/timeline/slavery.htm.

whom slavery had been ordained as a punishment.[4]

However, the northern soil and climate favored smaller farmsteads rather than large plantations. In the North between 1800 and 1860, the percentage of laborers working in agricultural pursuits dropped drastically. Only in New Jersey did a small minority continue to own slaves until the eve of the Civil War.

In the North, slavery was replaced in the cities and factories by immigrant labor from Europe. In fact, most immigrants, seven out of every eight, settled in the North rather than in the South. Industry flourished in the North, driven by their more abundant natural resources and a seemingly endless supply of immigrant labor.

In 1803, President Thomas Jefferson authorized the purchase of approximately 828,000,000 square miles of territory from France. The Louisiana Purchase as it became known doubled the size of the United States. The area purchased stretched from the Mississippi River in the east to the Rocky Mountains in the west and from the Gulf of Mexico in the south to the Canadian border in the north. In 1807, slave trade was abolished in America. With it no longer possible to import

---

[4] http://slavenorth.com/massachusetts.htm.

slaves, the major concern became the expansion of slavery into the new territories.

In 1819 Missouri applied for admission to the Union, the first section of the recently acquired Louisiana Territory to do so as a slave state. Tension was already high over the issue, and the admission of Missouri threatened to upset the delicate balance in Congress between slave states and the non-slave-holding states. The rapid growth in population in the North had left the Southern states, for the first time, with less than 45 percent of the seats in the U.S. House of Representatives. The U.S. Senate was evenly balanced between eleven slave and eleven non-slave-holding states. Therefore, Missouri's 1818 application for statehood, if approved, would give the slave states a majority in the Senate and reduce the Northern majority in the House. To keep the peace, Congress formulated a two-part compromise, granting Missouri's request but also admitting Maine as a free state. Furthermore, except for Missouri, this law prohibited slavery in the Louisiana Territory north of the 36° 30´ latitude line. This became known as the Missouri Compromise, the implications of which Thomas Jefferson considered as troubling as a "Firebell in the Night."

The 1791 territorial census of Tennessee showed a black population of 3,417, which was about 10 percent of the total population. Tennessee's slave population increased faster than the general population. By 1860, 24.8 percent of the population were African slaves. Though slaves were numerous, only 4.5 percent of the white population owned slaves even though 80 percent of southerners owned the land they tilled.[5]

In 1860 there were 63 slaveholders listed in Grundy County, Tennessee. A total of 266 slaves were listed on the census, the largest number being in Pelham Valley. There were 8 free colored males and 7 free colored females. The slave population included 115 males and 121 females. Only two individuals owned more than 30 slaves.

While large-scale slave auctions were not common in the county, slaves were sold or traded between local slave owners. This practice would provide much fodder for Abolitionists in their condemnation of slavery.

At the same time as the number of slaves was becoming more numerous in Tennessee, local movements began to arise encouraging the abolition of slavery. In 1819 Elihu Embree, the

---

[5] Tre Hargett, *Tennessee Blue Book* 2013-2014, 502, 511.

son of a Quaker minister who had moved from Pennsylvania, established the first newspaper in the United States devoted exclusively to freeing the slaves. Embree was a former slave owner who had freed his slaves some ten years earlier. Located in Jonesboro, TN, the *Manumission Intelligencer* later became known as the *Emancipator*.

The *Emancipator* advocated gradual emancipation and colonization of slaves. Soon East Tennessee would become a center of the abolitionist movement.[6]

The argument over slavery was long and complicated. Religious beliefs played a major role on both sides. Slaveholders claimed that the Bible sanctioned slavery, and it was the sacred duty of Christians to convert the "heathen race." After all, they argued, Abraham had slaves, and in the New Testament, Paul returned a runaway slave.

Who could question the Word of God when it said, "slaves, obey your earthly masters with fear and trembling" (Ephesians 6:5), or "tell slaves to be submissive to their masters and to give satisfaction in every respect" (Titus 2:9). Slavery, they contended,

---

[6] Ibid. 502.

was a natural state of mankind. The Greeks and Romans had owned slaves as well as many other civilizations.

Southerners contended that freeing the slaves would cause economic ruin to the South and the nation. The sudden end to the slave economy would have had a profound economic impact in the South where reliance on slave labor was the foundation of their economy. The cotton economy would collapse. The tobacco crop would dry in the fields without anyone to harvest it. Rice would cease being profitable. Unemployment would be rampant, which would lead to chaos and anarchy. Not only would it destroy the Southern economy, it would be detrimental to the slaves themselves. Many have argued that every war is, in essence, an economic war, and the American Civil War would be no different.

Abolitionists, on the other hand, thus deplored slavery as an evil institution that was cruel and inhumane and not at all in line with the teachings of Jesus. They denounced slavery as a sin and thus condemned the virtue of the South. Religious leaders on both sides joined the debate. The Quakers, who had long been opposed to slavery, led the movement.

Abolitionist Angelina Grimke wrote in her *Appeal to the*

Christian Women of the South that "It will be, and that very soon, clearly perceived and fully acknowledged by all the virtuous and the candid, that in principle it is as sinful to hold a human being in bondage who has been born in Carolina as one who has been born in Africa. All that sophistry [false logic] of argument which has been employed to prove that, although it is sinful to send to Africa to procure men and women as slaves who have never been in slavery, that still it is not sinful to keep those in bondage who have come down by inheritance, will be utterly over thrown. We must come back to the good old doctrine of our forefathers who declared to the world "this self-evident truth that all men are created equal, and that they have certain inalienable rights among which are, life, liberty, and the pursuit of happiness."[7]

    Religion played a major role in the war as well. Politicians on both sides invoked God as justification for their actions. In the South, religion proved to be the unifying force. The South, like the North, was convinced that God was on their side. The struggle might be one of David and Goliath, but God's side would prevail. Southerners viewed themselves as the "chosen"

---

[7] http://americainclass.org/wp-content/uploads/2013/06/Grimke_Appeal-to-the-ChristianWomen-of-the-South-excerpts.pdf.

people who had remained faithful to God while the North had abandoned the truths of God out of greed. Gradually, Southern sectionalism gave way to Southern nationalism.

At least 618,000 Americans died in the Civil War, and some experts say the toll reached 750,000. The number that is most often quoted is 620,000. An equivalent proportion of today's population would be about six million people. Confederate men died at a rate three times that of their Yankee counterparts; one in five Southern men of military age did not survive the Civil War.[8] These casualties exceed the nation's loss in all its other wars, from the Revolution through Vietnam. In both armies, more men died from sickness and disease than died in battle. One in thirteen who returned home had lost a limb. Civil War historians have estimated that as many as 50,000 civilians died during the war due to shortages of food, disease, and guerrilla attacks.

While records of all soldiers from Grundy County who fought in the Civil War are incomplete, the record of Turney's 1st Tennessee Infantry gives a glimpse into the devastation of war.

---

[8] Drew Gilpin Faust, *This Republic of Suffering*. (Knopf: New York, 2008) p. XI. Noted historian James McPherson and others place this as 1 out of 4 and possibly as high as 31%.

The company was comprised of men from Franklin, Coffee, and Grundy Counties. Of the 131 men about whom we have information, twelve men were killed in battle. Another 10 died because of illness or other causes. That brings the total killed or wounded to twenty-two, or 17 percent of the men. Thirty-eight of the men were wounded in battle, some of whom later died and are included in the list of the killed, bringing the total to 29 percent of the men wounded. Some were wounded more than once, and they are included for each time they were wounded.

Twenty-six of the men were taken prisoner; at least one more than once. The total number of prisoners of war came to 20 percent. Approximately 8 percent of the men were reported as deserters at one time or another. Many were on leave and were late returning to duty, possibly hampered by the Union occupation of Middle Tennessee. After Bragg's retreat from Tennessee in 1863, the number of deserters from Grundy County troops in Tennessee was probably much higher.

Alexander Houston Sanders provides an illustration of the life of a southern soldier. Sanders was born in Payne's Cove at the foot of the mountain near Pelham, Tennessee. He joined Turney's 1st Tennessee Regiment as a member of "The Pelham

Guard." He was shot in the arm at Harper's Ferry during the company's 1st engagement. He was promoted to 2nd Cpl. in October of 1862. He fought in the Battle of Gettysburg and was "authorized" to return home to raise a company. In March of 1864, he was considered a deserter. He managed to raise a Company and was appointed Captain of Company C of the 20th Tennessee Cavalry. He suffered a broken leg from a gunshot in Madison, Alabama, a wound to the chin in McMinnville, Tennessee, and a bullet wound to the thigh in Selma, Alabama, near the end of the war. He survived the war and returned to Grundy County where he was elected sheriff in 1892.[9]

At the outset of the war, neither army had organizations in place to handle the amount of death that the nation was about to experience. There were no national cemeteries, no burial details, and no emissaries to notify families of a death of a family member. The largest human devastation in American history, the Civil War forced the nation to face death and destruction in a way that has not been rivaled before or since.

---

[9] http://freepages.nostalgia.rootsweb.ancestry.com/~grundyconnections/bob bogle.html.

Recruitment of soldiers on both sides was highly localized throughout the war. Regiments would often be raised from the population of a few adjacent counties. Soldiers went to war with their neighbors and their kin. The nature of recruitment meant that a battlefield disaster could be a disaster for the home community. During the conflict, 2.1 million Northern troops, including 180,000 African Americans, and 880,000 Southerners, took up arms.[10]

Causes of War

The cause of the Civil War has long been debated. Defenders of the South have often cited states' rights as a primary cause. The doctrine of states' rights is based on the Tenth Amendment to the Constitution, which states, "The powers not delegated to the United States by the Constitution, nor prohibited by it to the states, are reserved to the states respectively, or to the people." From the time of the signing of the Constitution, the philosophy of states' rights has generated controversy. The Federalists, led by Alexander Hamilton, championed a strong central government deriving its authority from implied as well as express powers contained in the Constitution. The Jeffersonian Democrats advocated a "strict constructionists" stance that insisted all powers not specifically granted the federal government be reserved to the states. Ultimately, the proslavery states used states' rights doctrines to justify their secession.

The South was not the first to suggest the idea of secession. The earliest proponents of the idea were New England Federalists. From 1800 to 1815, there were three serious attempts at secession organized by New England Federalists, who believed that the policies of the Jefferson and Madison administrations, especially the 1803 Louisiana Purchase, the national embargo of 1807, and the War of 1812, were so detrimental to New England that they justified secession.

Prominent New Englanders voiced their support for states' rights. "I will rather anticipate a new confederacy, exempt from the corrupt and corrupting influence and oppression of the aristocratic Democrats of the South," wrote the well-known Massachusetts Federalist politician and U.S. Senator, Timothy Pickering, in 1803.

"The Northern States must be governed by Virginia or must govern Virginia, and there is no middle ground," cautioned Aaron Burr, who joined the New England Federalists in a secessionist plot.[10]

The origins of the Civil War can be traced back to the Declaration of Independence and beyond. From the founding of the United States, the idea of Manifest Destiny had been proposed by those who were anxious to expand the borders of the existing country. Proponents of Manifest Destiny thought it was the God-given right for the United States to control the land

---

[10] http://www.ditext.com/dilorenzo/yankee.html.

between the Atlantic and Pacific Oceans. Some had their designs on Mexico and Central America as well as Cuba. When war broke out in 1846 between the U.S. and Mexico, some saw that as a pretext for U.S. expansion. President James K. Polk was a native of Tennessee and a slaveholder. Many in the North viewed "Polk's War" as an excuse to expand slavery. The territory taken from Mexico during the war would become a battleground for free-soilers and advocates of slavery. Many solutions were proposed for how to handle the territory, but the territory remained an area of contention for both sides.

Despite their rhetoric, it is generally understood that southern states fought to maintain their economy, which was agricultural and based upon the institution of slavery. "Had there been no slavery, there would have been no war. Had there been no moral condemnation of slavery, there would have been no war."[11]

The first black African slaves in the American colonies also arrived during the early 1600's, and the slave population

---

[11] This observation was made by Sydney E. Ahlstrome, in his monumental study of religion in America, *A Religious History of the American People*, (New Haven: Yale University Press, 1972), p. 649; it was echoed by Maj. General John B. Gordon, CSA, in his Memoirs, Chapter 1, p.1.

increased rapidly during the 1700's. By 1750, about 200,000 slaves lived in the colonies. The majority lived in the South, where the warm climate and fertile soil encouraged the development of plantations that grew rice, tobacco, sugar cane, and later cotton. Most plantation slaves worked in the fields. Some were craft workers and house servants.

Slavery increased rapidly in the South after Eli Whitney of Massachusetts invented his cotton gin in 1793. The cotton gin removed the seeds from cotton as fast as 50 people working by hand, thus permitting the planters to cultivate much more of the crop. This required a larger work force. The work was exhausting, and few white workers were interested in backbreaking work for meager pay. The answer was to use slaves. By using slave labor, farmers could meet the rapidly escalating demand for cotton. The South grew three-quarters of the world's marketed cotton. As a result, the Southern cotton industry flourished, and cotton became the chief crop in the region. The planters needed more and more workers to pick and bale the cotton, which led to an increase in the slave population. By 1860, about 4 million slaves lived in the South. Cotton increased the need for slaves and the price of workers continued to rise. By 1860, slaves were the primary source of wealth in the South.

With the slave population so large, there was a constant fear of revolt. Nat Turner's Rebellion took place in Virginia in August 1831 and created a great deal of alarm among southern whites. Nat Turner and a group of rebel slaves killed 65 people. Turner claimed that God had instructed him to kill whites in order to gain his freedom. The violence and fear triggered by this event brought about a stricter control of the slave population. Turner's rebellion revealed that slaves were not happy in the plantation system as some defenders of slavery claimed. This strengthened the abolitionist movement and proved to be a catalyst to further action.

Sectionalism intensified between 1800 and 1860. The North phased out slavery and became more industrialized while the Southern economy centered around plantation agriculture that was dependent on slave labor. Cotton prices were high, and the Southern economy thrived.

Northern industry, still in its developmental stage, could not equal Europe's factory system. Northern interests favored a tariff to enable them to compete with the European manufacturers. Southerners who had little manufacturing capacity imported most of their manufactured products and opposed the tariff because it increased the price on imported goods. The Tariff of 1828 increased the tax rate on imported products to 40 percent. It was known as the Tariff of Abominations in the South and was widely denounced by southern states. South Carolina attempted to nullify the Tariff of 1828 with vows to leave the Union. President Andrew Jackson acted quickly to preserve the Union, threatening to hang anyone who followed through with the attempted disunion.

Though temporarily solved by a compromise proposed by Henry Clay, the issues which arose over tariffs continued to divide the North and South, as did the expansion of slavery into new territories. It soon became obvious that whoever controlled these new territories would control the tariff issue and determine the fate of slavery.

Contributing to the general unrest was the emergence of what became known as the Underground Railroad. The Underground Railroad was the expression used to describe a network of meeting places, secret routes, passageways and safe houses used by slaves in the U.S. to escape slave states to northern states and Canada.

The Underground Railroad helped thousands of slaves escape bondage. By one estimate, 100,000 slaves escaped the South between 1810 and 1850. Harriet Tubman, the most famous "conductor" of the Underground Railroad, is said to have made 13 trips into the South to free slaves. Quaker Levi Coffin and his wife Catherine are believed to have aided over 2,000 slaves to escape over a period of years, making them the most successful conductors on the Underground Railroad.[12]

Abolitionists were determined to free as many slaves as possible, even though such actions violated state laws and the United States Constitution. Lawmen sent to retrieve runaways were often attacked and beaten by abolitionist mobs. To the slave holding states, this suggested that Northerners wanted to choose which parts of the Constitution they would enforce, while expecting the South to honor the entire document.

The union of states came close to splitting again in 1850. The Northern abolitionists led by William Lloyd Garrison made a push to separate from the slave holding states. In 1854, he publicly burned a copy of the Constitution because it permitted

---

[12] http://www.ohiohistorycentral.org/w/Levi_Coffin.

slavery. He called for the North to secede from the Union to sever the ties with the slaveholding south. In the South, John C. Calhoun was proclaiming that "disunion is the only alternative that is left for us."[13]

With the acquisition of a huge new territory in the West, gained by our victory over Mexico in 1849, the issue of sectional balance in the Congress again became an issue. When California asked for statehood as a free state, it seemed certain that the union was about to dissolve. Henry Clay managed to diffuse the crisis. Clay ran five times for president and was the best-known political figure in the county. With the help of Daniel Webster, a distinguished New England statesman and an avowed anti-slave champion, Henry Clay was able to push through Congress what became known as the Compromise of 1850.

The Compromise of 1850 allowed California to be admitted to the union as a free state, called for a strict Fugitive Slave Law, and, most importantly, allowed for new territories in the southwest to become states without restrictions on slavery. Abolitionists were angry at Webster and depicted him as a

---

[13] John F. Kennedy, *Profiles in Courage* (Harper: New York and London, 1956), 63.

traitor. For Webster, the matter was simple. The Union must be preserved at all costs. Clay, who had earned the reputation as the "Great Compromiser," was a force in American government for forty years, and he and Webster united to prevent the dissolution of the Union. Ten years later both would be gone, and no one of their stature and influence was present to prevent the country from going to war. Senator Henry S. Foote of Mississippi would later write, "Had there been one such man in the Congress of the United States as Henry Clay in 1860-1861 there would, I feel sure, have been no civil war."[14]

Historian Charles Beard has labeled the dispute between slavery and freedom in the words of New York Senator William Seward, as an "Irrepressible Conflict." Seward wrote during the presidential campaign of 1860 in South Carolina that "The irrepressible conflict is about to be visited upon us through the Black Republican nominee and his fanatical, diabolical Republican party." Seward meant that the United States must choose to be entirely a slave holding nation or a free nation. It was a conflict that was unavoidable.

---

[14] Robert Remini, *Henry Clay Statesman for the Union* (New York: WW Norton and Company, 1993), pp. 761-762.

Beard argued that slavery was not, as many believe, the fundamental issue leading up to the Civil War, but rather, it was one of the many reasons that led America toward war. Few historians today would agree in principle with Beard. While many factors played a role in the war occurring when it did, few would argue that slavery was not the primary cause. At the time however, many Southerners agreed with former president James Buchanan that it was a "needless war," caused primarily by the work of fanatical antislavery agitators in the North."[15]

During the 1850's, a series of events further divided the nation. Southern slave owners felt that their rights and interests were no longer being fairly represented. Northerners began to increasingly support free soil and even abolition, so tensions between the two sections intensified until Southerners became convinced that nothing short of secession could protect them from Northern persecution.

In 1852, Harriet Beecher Stowe attacked slavery in her novel *Uncle Tom's Cabin*. Stowe, a Northern abolitionist outraged by the Fugitive Slave Law, wrote a novel to illustrate the evils of slavery.

---

[15] Edwin Rozwenc, Ed. *The Causes of the American Civil War*. (Lexington: DC Heath and Company, 1961),24.

Though overly sentimental and condescending in her descriptions of the book's black characters, *Uncle Tom's Cabin* was the top-selling American novel in the 19th century. The novel cemented Northern opinion against slavery. Even though Stowe had never been in the South, the stereotypes of African Americans and harsh slave owners were generally accepted in the North. *Uncle Tom's Cabin* was described by poet Langston Hughes as the most "cussed and discussed book" of its time.[16]

Another important change in the political landscape came with the Kansas-Nebraska Act of 1854 that mandated "popular sovereignty," allowing settlers of a territory to decide whether slavery would be allowed within a new state's borders. Proposed by Stephen A. Douglas, the bill overturned the Missouri Compromise's use of latitude as the boundary between slave and free territory.

In 1854, Douglas had introduced a bill to organize the territory of Nebraska to bring the area under civil control. Douglas's motive was to ensure a northern transcontinental railroad route that would benefit his home state of Illinois.

---

[16] https://ap.gilderlehrman.org/essays/uncletom%C3%A2%E2%82%AC%E2%84%A2s-cabinand-matter-influence.

Southern senators objected; the region lay north of latitude 36°30′, so under the terms of the Missouri Compromise of 1820, it would become a free state. To gain the southerners' support, Douglas proposed creating two territories—Kansas and Nebraska—effectively repealing the Missouri Compromise line. The question of whether the territories would be slave or free would be left to the settlers under Douglas's principle of popular sovereignty. Presumably, the more Northern territory would oppose slavery while the more Southern one would permit it.

The Kansas-Nebraska Act proved to be one of the most important catalysts leading to the Civil War. Proponents from pro-slavery and free-soil factions battled for control of the territory. The subsequent rash of violence gave rise to the term "Bleeding Kansas" and propelled the country closer to civil war.

The Dred Scott decision also had a major impact on the abolitionist movement. At the heart of the case was the most important question of the 1850's: Should slavery be allowed in the West? As part of the Kansas settlement, residents of newly created territories could decide the issue of slavery by vote. When it was applied in Kansas in 1854, however, violence erupted.

Dred Scott was born around 1800 in Virginia. He journeyed westward with his master, Peter Blow, first to Alabama and then, in 1830, to St. Louis, Missouri. Two years later Peter Blow died. Scott was then purchased by Army surgeon Dr. John Emerson. Emerson took Scott to the free state of Illinois. In the spring of 1836, after a stay of two and a half years, Emerson moved to a fort in the Wisconsin Territory. While there, Scott met and married Harriet Robinson, a slave owned by a local justice of the peace. Ownership of Harriet was transferred to Emerson.

Scott felt that his stay in Illinois, a free state, gave him the legal standing to petition for freedom, as did his time in Wisconsin, where slavery was also prohibited. Scott tried to buy his freedom, but his offer was refused. With abolitionist backing as a test case, Scott then sought freedom through the courts claiming his time as a resident of a free state made him free.

Scott went to trial in June of 1847 but lost on a technicality. In 1848, the Missouri Supreme Court decided that the case should be retried. In an 1850 retrial, the St Louis circuit court ruled that Scott and his family were free. Two years later the Missouri Supreme Court reversed the decision of the lower court. Scott then brought his case to a federal court, the United States Circuit

Court in Missouri. In 1854, the Circuit Court upheld the decision of the Missouri Supreme Court. Scott appealed this decision to the United States Supreme Court.

The nine justices of the Supreme Court of 1856 certainly had biases regarding slavery. Seven had been appointed by pro-slavery presidents from the South, and of these, five were from slave-holding families.

The decision of the court was read in March of 1857. Chief Justice Roger B. Taney—a staunch supporter of slavery—wrote the "majority opinion" for the court. It stated that because Scott was black, he was not a citizen and therefore had no right to sue. In what is perhaps the most infamous case in its history, the court ruled that all people of African ancestry—slaves as well as those who were free—could never become citizens of the United States and therefore, could not sue in federal court. The court also ruled that the federal government did not have the power to prohibit slavery in its territories.

While the decision was well received by slaveholders in the South, many Northerners were outraged. This decision greatly influenced the nomination of Abraham Lincoln as the Republican candidate for president in 1860 and his subsequent election, which in turn, led to the South's secession from the Union.

Peter Blow's sons, childhood friends of Scott, had helped pay Scott's legal fees through the years. After the Supreme Court's decision, the former master's sons purchased Scott and his wife and set them free. Dred Scott died nine months later.

In 1859, infuriated by the Dred Scott case and the violence against free-soilers in Kansas, abolitionist John Brown led a raid on the U.S. arsenal at Harpers Ferry in Virginia. Brown was already infamous for his role in a massacre of Southern settlers that took place in Pottawatomie, Kansas. He was also a friend of prominent abolitionists Harrier Tubman and Fredrick Douglass. Brown's plan was to seize weapons from the federal arsenal and start a slave uprising. The slaves failed to respond, and Brown remained in Harper's Ferry instead of escaping into the mountains as he had planned. He was captured and convicted of treason. He proved to be prophetic as he said on the way to the gallows on December 2, 1859, "[I] am now quite certain that the crimes of this guilty land will never be purged away; but with blood."[17] Brown was hanged, and after his death, he was viewed as a martyr for the abolitionist cause. The South could never understand how the North could view a murderer and robber in such high regard. Brown's raid further divided the North and the South and paved the way for secession. "By 1860 . . . southern whites lived in mortal terror of abolitionist-led slave revolts."[18]

The final event that led to secession was the presidential election of 1860. The Democratic Party was divided, and a united Republican Party appealed solely to the Northern states to win the campaign. They had nominated Abraham Lincoln, a respected state politician in Illinois, who held a moderate view on slavery.

Lincoln came to national prominence during his failed bid for the Illinois senate in 1858. Though Lincoln lost the election, his series of debates with Stephen Douglas enhanced his

---

[17] David S. Reynolds, *John Brown, Abolitionist: The Man Who Killed Slavery, Sparked the Civil War, and Seceded Civil Rights* (New York: Random House, 2005), 395.

[18] Stephen V. Ash, *When the Yankees Came*. (Chapel Hill and London: The University of North Carolina Press: 1995),10.

reputation among those opposed to slavery.

Lincoln disliked slavery but was not an abolitionist. He believed slavery to be a moral evil. In one of his most famous speeches he had said, "A house divided against itself cannot stand. I believe this government cannot endure permanently half-slave and half free. I do not expect the Union to be dissolved - I do not expect the house to fall - but I do expect it will cease to be divided. It will become all one thing or all the other."[19]

Later, he explained his expectations: "I do not wish to be misunderstood upon this subject of slavery in this country. I suppose it may long exist, and perhaps the best way for it to come to an end peaceably is for it to exist for a length of time. But I say that the spread and strengthening and perpetuation of it is an entirely different proposition. There we should in every way resist it as a wrong, treating it as a wrong, with the fixed idea that it must and will come to an end."[20]

---

[19] "Lincoln's 'House-Divided' Speech in Springfield, Illinois, June 16, 1858. The House Divided analogy was first used in reference to the Whig Party being divided.

[20] Roy P. Basler, Ed. *The Collected Works of Abraham Lincoln*, Volume III, "Speech at Chicago, Illinois" March 1, 1859 (Camden: Rutgers University Press, 1953), 370.

Southern elements insisted that the nominating convention make a strong statement supporting slavery in the territories by nominating John C. Breckinridge, who was descended from an old Kentucky family and was distinguished in law and politics. At 36, he had been the youngest vice president in American history.

Western Democrats, however, opposed that stance and endorsed Stephen A. Douglas, a proponent of popular sovereignty. The Democrats thus nominated two candidates. The Constitutional Union Party, a coalition of Whigs and Unionists, nominated Tennessean John Bell, who, although a slave owner, opposed the expansion of slavery and campaigned vigorously against secession. Grundy County, which had voted Democratic in every election since its inception, continued the trend by voting overwhelmingly for Breckinridge.

The Republican Party's success was constructed on its opposition to the spread of slavery. It opposed the expansion of slavery and called upon Congress to take steps, whenever necessary, to prevent its extension. Southerners thought that by confining slavery within its present boundaries, the institution would be placed on the road to eventual extinction.

The Democratic candidates split the votes, and Abraham Lincoln became the 16th president of the United States. He tried to alleviate the fears of Southerners in his first inaugural address:

Apprehension seems to exist among the people of the Southern States that by the accession of a Republican Administration their property and their peace and personal security are to be endangered. There has never been any reasonable cause for such apprehension. Indeed, the most ample evidence to the contrary has all the while existed and been open to their inspection. It is found in nearly all the published speeches of him who now addresses you. I do but quote from one of those speeches when I declare that- **I have no purpose, directly or indirectly, to interfere with the institution of slavery in the States where it exists.** *I believe I have no lawful right to do so, and I have no inclination to do so.*[21]

---

[21] Abraham Lincoln's 1st Inaugural Address, March 4, 1861. Washington, DC.

Despite the consensus among modern day historians that slavery was the cause of the Civil War, questions remain. The origins of slavery in the United States had roots in the North as well as in the South. Many of the early slave traders had New England origins. Southern cotton fueled northern textile manufacturing, and a major portion of the federal revenue came from the southern export trade. Therefore, the future of American industry rested on the economic stability of the South.

Though many abolitionists espoused the belief that the slaves needed to be freed, few white people in the North and West wanted them as equals or as a part of their society. Many states even outlawed free blacks from moving into their territory. In fact, racist attitudes were as common in the North as in the South. Lincoln in his debate with Stephen Douglas in 1858 said, "I will say then that I am not, nor have I ever been in favor of bringing about in any way the social and political equality of the white and black races . . . there is a physical difference between the white and black races which I believe will forever forbid the two races living together on terms of social and political equality."[22]

---

[22] Lincoln-Douglas Debate, September 18, 1858.

What plans did the North have for slaves once they were free? Lincoln confessed that he did not have the answers as to what to do to solve the questions of free Negroes. Though fewer in number in the North, blacks were segregated more strictly than in the South. Many northerners were blatant racists who might have a moral objection to slavery but had no intention of treating the slaves as equals. So, what was to be done with the slaves if they were freed?

In the South, where African Americans made up a large percent of the population, slavery was a means of racial control and white supremacy. With 95 percent of the black population living in the South, this was a major concern. For many in the North, preventing the spread of slavery was a form of racial segregation, and not always motivated by any altruistic ideals. Much of the rhetoric over the spread of slavery to new territories was simply a method to prevent African Americans from settling in Northern and Western territories.

For President Lincoln, especially early in the war, slavery was not his main concern as he explained in a letter to Horace Greely in August of 1862. "My paramount objective in this struggle is to save the Union, and is not either to save or destroy slavery ... What I do about slavery and the colored race, I do because I believe it helps to save the Union."[23]

Still, it seems an odd statement given the circumstances. President Lincoln was willing to save the Union at the cost of more than one half a million lives without freeing the slaves.

Why was he not willing to find a peaceful, morally acceptable way to save the Union and free the slaves? In 1861, no national party proposed the idea of emancipation and integrating the African population into American life.

---

[23] Letter, Abraham Lincoln to Horace Greely, August 22, 1862.

Birth of the Confederacy

Despite Lincoln's assurance, South Carolina called a convention to discuss seceding from the Union before Lincoln was inaugurated. On December 24, 1860, South Carolina adopted a declaration of secession and left the Union. Six other southern states quickly followed. On February 4, 1861, a convention with representatives from South Carolina, Mississippi, Florida, Alabama, Georgia, Louisiana, and Texas met in Montgomery, Alabama. The Montgomery Convention marked the formal beginning of the Confederate States of America. The convention organized a provisional government for the Confederacy and created the Constitution of the Confederate States.

The Convention appointed Jefferson Davis of Mississippi as provisional president and Alexander Stephens of Georgia as vice-president. The Convention also set dates for a formal election for these offices; both Davis and Stephens were then elected without opposition.

In 1845, Davis had been elected to the U.S. House of Representatives. He resigned in June 1846, to command a Mississippi regiment in the Mexican War. Under Zachary Taylor he distinguished himself both at the siege of Monterrey and at Buena Vista. In 1847, Davis was appointed U.S. Senator from Mississippi to fill an unexpired term but resigned in 1851 to run for governor of Mississippi against his senatorial colleague, Henry S. Foote. Davis was a strong champion of Southern rights and argued for the expansion of slave territory and economic development of the South to counterbalance the power of the North. He lost the election by less than a thousand votes and retired to his plantation until appointed (1853) Secretary of War by Franklin Pierce. Reentering the Senate in 1857, Davis became the leader of the Southern block.

Davis took little part in the secession movement until Mississippi seceded (Jan. 1861), whereupon he withdrew from the Senate. He was immediately appointed major general of the Mississippi militia, and shortly afterward, he was chosen president of the Confederate provisional government established by the convention at Montgomery, Alabama. He was inaugurated at Richmond, Va., in February of 1862.[24]

A month before the Civil War broke out the Confederate government took steps to raise a militia. Soldiers were originally

---

[24] http://www.us-civilwar.com/davis.htm.

enlisted for 12 months service. The act of March 6, 1861, that organized these forces also provided for the establishment of the Army of the Confederate States of America, a counterpart to the U.S. Army. At the outset, Confederate officials projected this regular force to number about 10,000 officers and men, a figure that President Jefferson Davis later cited as proof that "the wish and policy" of his government "was peace." He explained, "I worked night and day for twelve years to prevent the war, but I could not. The North was mad and blind, would not let us govern ourselves, and so the war came."[25]

Davis chose Joseph E. Johnston, a career U.S. Army officer, who served with distinction in the Mexican-American War and Seminole Wars as commander of the Confederate Army. Johnston was wounded in the spring of 1862 fighting at the Battle of Seven Pines in Virginia. He was replaced by Robert E. Lee, who led the Army of Northern Virginia for the remainder of the war. Upon his recovery, Johnston was given charge of a largely supervisory command entitled the Department of the West, placing him in charge of Braxton Bragg's Army of Tennessee.

---

[25] http://www.americancivilwarstory.com/jefferson-davis-quotes.html.

In 1861, Robert E. Lee, the son of Revolutionary War hero "Light-Horse Harry" Lee and a graduate of West Point, was an army officer serving in Texas. When he heard Texas had left the Union, he insisted that secessionists would have to fight him to get Federal property. He anticipated that his native Virginia would remain in the Union, allowing him to remain loyal to his state and nation. He was recalled from Texas, and Lincoln promoted him to full colonel of First Regiment of Cavalry. Lee accepted, swearing allegiance to the Union.[26]

Lincoln planned to offer Lee command of the entire Union Army, but in April of 1861, Virginia joined the Confederacy. Lee was at a moment of crisis. Even though he saw nothing but "anarchy and ruin" in secession, he could not bring himself to raise a hand against his home and his heritage. Lee chose to follow his home state, despite his personal desire for the country to remain intact and even though President Abraham Lincoln had offered him command of a Union Army.[27]

---

[26] Elizabeth Brown Pryor, "Robert E. Lee's Severest Struggle" American Heritage:, 22.

[27] Ibid 23.

Lee was placed in charge of the conduct of military operations in the armies of the Confederacy on March 13, 1862. He was referred to as Davis' military adviser but exercised broad control over the strategic and logistical aspects of the Army, a role similar in nature to the current Chief of Staff of the United States Army. On June 1, he assumed command of the Army of Northern Virginia, which was considered the most important of all the Confederate field armies. This was the result of the serious wounds suffered by Joseph E. Johnston during the Seven Days campaign.

Emotions in the South were at a fever pitch. Politicians and newspapers fanned the flames of secession. On January 9, 1861, an editorial in the *Nashville Daily Gazette* summarized the secessionist view of the conflict. *"We cannot see how any Southern man, who is at all familiar with the history of the times, can . . . solemnly declare it inexpedient for the people of his State to hold a convention and determine whether they will resist or submit to the Abolition rule now about to be inaugurated. . . . Tennessee will resist."*[28]

---

[28] *Nashville Daily Gazette* January 9, 1861.

When the Civil War began in 1861, most Americans were sure the war would not last very long and there would be few casualties. Individuals were caught up in the emotions as well though few expected the horror of war. Senator James Chesnut, Jr., promised to drink any blood spilled. After all, "a lady's thimble," as a common saying had it, "will hold all the blood that will be shed"[29] because of secession. He could not foresee the degree of the death and destruction that would occur.

Others shared a similar sentiment, one that was probably shared by many in Grundy County. A Tennessee native would write:

"Yes, we are all for fighting. Everybody is willing – even the ladies.... I think there is enough patriotism & bravery in this state to sustain the Southern Confederacy against the United States troops and all the Yankees who dare accompany them.... The South will never unite with the North again – never."[30]

The boarder states were torn between remaining loyal to the Union and supporting their sister states to the South. In

---

[29] http://news.nationalgeographic.com/news/2011/04/110411-civil-war-150th-anniversaryfort-sumter-battle/.

December 1860, Tennessee governor Isham G. Harris convened the general assembly in Nashville. To get a better view of voter's sentiments, the Legislature called for a referendum to decide whether a secession convention should be held. Governor Harris enumerated twenty-three complaints against the North. East Tennessee was strongly opposed to secession. William G."Parsons" Brownlow of Knoxville wrote in his influential paper *The Whig*, "We have no parties but Union men and Disunionists."[31]

On January 7, 1861, Tennessee Governor Isham Harris called the Legislature into session to adopt a resolution asking Tennesseans to vote for or against a convention to consider the possibility of secession. He recommends the organization of a state militia and the purchase of arms, and states that "the remedy for the present evils exists only in constitutional amendments." The convention was voted down by more than 10,000 votes: 69,675 to 57,798. Union sentiment was especially strong in mountainous areas, and voters rejected the referendum

---

[30] From *a January 24, 1861, letter of W.W. Fergusson, Riddleton, TN*] www.Tennessee.gov/tsla/.../Timelines/1861%20Timeline.doc.

[31] Oliver Temple, *East Tennessee and the Civil War*, (Knoxville: Overmountain Press, 1995), 171.

by a 54-46% margin (over 80% of East Tennesseans voted against it). Grundy County voted 393 for a convention, and 58 opposed to a convention.[32] Most of the surrounding counties (Marion, Van Buren, and Bledsoe) on the Cumberland Plateau voted against a convention. Though Tennesseans opposed the election of Lincoln, they took a wait-and-see attitude, believing that he had been legally elected, and his election alone was not enough to force them to leave the Union.

Governor Harris was still determined to lead Tennessee out of the Union. A native of Franklin County, Tennessee, he lived until age 14 near Estill Springs. He was educated at Carrick Academy, a state-chartered school in Winchester, which was in operation from 1809 until 1878 and offered mainly high school education for boys, but also had some "primary" and "grammar" male students. Led by Harris, Franklin County had voted in favor of secession 1,240 to 206, though the majority of the state did not agree.

---

[32] *Nashville Union and American*, March 3, 1861.

Upset at the vote, the citizens of Franklin County, which borders Alabama, held mass meetings in protest to the vote. Peter Turney offered a resolution declaring that the people of Franklin County were compelled by a vote to remain in the Union "against our wills and earnest desires, when our hearts, sympathies, and feelings are with the Confederate States of America."[33]

Turney was born in Jasper, Tennessee. Shortly after his birth, the Turney family moved to Winchester, Tennessee. He attended public schools in Franklin County and a private school in Nashville and read law, initially, with his father and later (after his father was elected to the Senate) with Judge W.E. Venable. After his admission to the bar in 1848, he practiced in Winchester.[34]

By spring of 1861, secession seemed inevitable. Southern politicians extolled the virtues of the South and exaggerated the evils of the North. The idea of Yankees invading the South, killing, stealing, and burning, was used to incite the feelings of

---

[33] Stanley F. Horn, *Tennessee's War: 1861-1865*, (Tennessee Civil War Centennial Commission, Nashville, 1965),15.

[34] Leonard Schlup, "Peter Turney," *Tennessee Encyclopedia of History and Culture*, 2009, Retrieved: 15 November 2012.

the people. "The possibility of war caused little gloom, especially among secessionists whose thinking was so dominated by the idea of 'going to' war that the possibility of war 'coming to' them was scarcely considered. . . . This would be a short affair somewhere in Virginia in which one Southerner would whip five Yankees and all the Southern soldiers would return home genuine heroes."[35]

Both sides added momentum in April when Federal forces tried to resupply Fort Sumter, a Union held fortress in South Carolina. On April 12, 1861, General P.G.T. Beauregard, in command of the Confederate forces around Charleston Harbor, opened fire on the Union garrison occupying Fort Sumter. On April 13, Major Robert Anderson, garrison commander, surrendered the fort and it was evacuated the next day.

Northerners were stunned, frightened, and outraged by the attack on the American fort. It was treason and nothing else in the minds of the North. Compromise and reason had failed. Now, the only thing that was left was to suppress the rebellion and subdue the South.

---

[35] Bob Womack, *Call Forth the Mighty Men*, (Bessemer: Colonial Press, 1987), p. 13.

Much debate has been generated as to why the Confederate government sanctioned the attack on Fort Sumter. Lincoln, in a skillful political maneuver, was careful not to be the aggressor. He forced the Confederate hand by warning South Carolina that he was sending in supplies to his besieged men inside the fort and that he would retaliate against any attack on the fort or those supplying it. If the Confederate government allowed the fort to be resupplied, they appeared weak. If they attacked the fort, they would incite Unionist sentiment in the North.

By attacking first, the Confederates were branded by those in the North as aggressors and not just defenders of their homeland. Clearly, from the southern point of view, the North became the aggressor when they tried to resupply the fort; however, the opening volley cast the South in an antagonistic role. Many people opposed the use of force to keep states in the Union.

By firing on the American flag at Fort Sumter, the South aroused and united the North. Without Fort Sumter, it would have been difficult for President Lincoln to acquire enough support to declare war on the Southern states to preserve the

Union. The South might have won their independence peacefully as many had predicted.

However, from the beginning of his presidency, Lincoln rejected the idea of letting the southern states withdraw from the Union peacefully. He believed that secession was illegal and that the use of force against the Federal Government was rebellion and treason against the United States. He refused to recognize the Confederate States as an official government and would not allow anyone in his administration to negotiate with their representatives.

In March 1861, Jefferson Davis sent peace commissioners to Washington with an offer to pay for all Federal property in the South and to take on the Southern portion of the national debt. However, Lincoln refused even to acknowledge the envoys, thus blocking any attempt to resolve the conflict by peaceful means. He took the hard line that the Southern states must return to the Union. It became inevitable that the two sides would fight.[36]

---

[36] http://www.san.beck.org/LincolnCivilWar.html.

Tennessee 1861

When Governor Harris call for a vote to decide whether the Tennessee's legislature should meet to vote on the secession issue, Tennessee voters rejected the plan and upheld the state's ties to the Union, though 87 percent of the citizens of Grundy County voted for a convention to decide if Tennessee should leave the Union. As a result, Peter Turney spearheaded a movement that called for Franklin County to secede from Tennessee and join Alabama. On April 15, 1861, President Lincoln called for 75,000 to volunteer for three months to put down the rebellion. He appealed to all loyal citizens in every state to preserve the Union.

Lincoln's call for troops to put down the rebellion in the South was the spark needed to convince those with undecided opinions to join the Confederacy. Southerners felt bound by honor and duty to protect their families and homes from invaders. Tennessee governor Isham Harris responded by saying, "The State of Tennessee will furnish no troops for the subjugation of the South, but 50,000 to resist coercion of its people."[37]

---

[37] Tennessee Governor Isham Harris in response to Abraham Lincoln's request for troops to put down the rebellion.

White County, Tennessee native Amanda McDowell wrote prophetically in her diary on May 4th, 1861: "The Southerners are so hot they can stand it no longer and have already made the break. There will be many a divided family in this once happy Union. There will be father against son and brother against brother. O, God that this should be in a Christian land. That men in their blindness should rush so rashly to ruin, and not only rush to ruin themselves but drag with them so many thousands of innocent and ignorant victims!"[38]

Led by Governor Harris, who one East Tennessee newspaper said was "more deserving of [the] gallows than Benedict Arnold,"[39] the Tennessee legislature brought about another referendum calling for secession. On June 8, 1861, secession was approved by vote of 104,913 to 47,238, although roughly 70 percent of East Tennesseans still voted against it. State Senator Edward J. Wood, representing Grundy County, was a strong supporter of secession, as was Grundy County's representative in the state house, J. M. Shields.

---

[38] Amanda McDowell, *Fiddles in the Cumberland*. (New York: Richard R. Smith, 1943) 45.

[39] Phillip Hamer, *Tennessee: A History*, (New York: American Historical Society, Inc. 1933) 508.

Once again Grundy County voted in favor of secession by a margin of 528 to 9. Why did Grundy County vote differently from most areas on the plateau? What was responsible for this anomaly? Dr. Michael Bradley has pointed out that Grundy County had a railroad spur, and the primary product shipped on the railroad lines was coal, much of which went to the southern states. Studies of Kentucky and Tennessee have shown that the presence of two or more large slave owners in an area often influenced the secession vote.[40]

Pelham, Tarleton Valley, and Hubbard's Cove are in the valley, and the largest slaveholders in Grundy County in 1860 lived there. Alexander Patton of Pelham owned 31 slaves valued at $22,300. His personal wealth was listed at $47,291 with a property value of $38,400. John Armfield was listed as owning 32 slaves, and his personal wealth was listed at $201,760 with a property value of $15,000, according to the 1860 census.

Historian Aaron Astor points out that "local elites were especially important in consolidating and defending certain ideological positions, and the vast majority of middling and poor

---

[40] Authors interview with Dr. Michael Bradley, May 2014.

residents took their cues from these powerful neighbors."[41] Large numbers of non-slave owners followed the lead of the planter class as they traditionally did. Coupled with the fear of what freedom for blacks would mean to the yeoman class, they chose to follow their "betters" and vote for secession.

Another possibility could have been the result of secessionist fever that pervaded much of the South. Amanda McDowell from nearby White County, Tennessee described events there: "Yesterday was the great election day in Tennessee. I guess it is voted out of the Union' by this time. But it would not have been had the people been able to vote their true sentiments. . . . Nearly all the Union men in the neighborhood stayed at home, not wishing to get into a brawl and deeming it a hopeless cause."[42]

There were Union men at the voting precincts, but "none of them ventured near to vote for fear of their lives." She continued to lament the loss of freedom: "A man dares not speak his

---

[41] Aaron Astor, *The Civil War Along the Cumberland Plateau.* (Charleston: The History Press, 2015), 64. Quoted from Martin Crawford, *Ashe County's Civil War: Community and Society in the Appalachian South.*

[42] Amanda McDowell, *Fiddles in the Cumberland.* (New York: Richard R. Smith, 1945) 49,181.

thoughts these days, unless he happened to be in accordance with the views of the Dictators. But I hope the time will yet come when an honest man can think what he pleases and speak his thoughts too."[43]

The Union men of Tennessee were determined not to give up the state without a fight. East Tennessee leaders met in Greeneville, Tennessee and delegates drafted a petition asking that the Tennessee state government allow pro-Union East Tennessee counties to form a separate state that would remain a part of the United States. State troops were sent to East Tennessee to put down any insurrection. Historian Stanley Horn has suggested that "Tennessee never seceded; Isham G. Harris seceded and carried Tennessee with him."[44]

In East Tennessee, Confederate leaders began to exert their power against the largely unorganized Union faction. Many within the Confederate border refused to support the Confederate government and some worked to undermine it. Some Union sympathizers left their homes and fled to Kentucky.

---

[43] Amanda McDowell, *Fiddles in the Cumberland*. (New York: Richard R. Smith, 1945) 49, 181.

[44] Stanley F. Horn, *The Army of Tennessee* (Wilmington NC.; Broadfoot Publishing, 1987), 47.

Union men were charged with disloyalty, and neighbors who had once lived agreeably now became bitter enemies. Family members became estranged and took opposing sides.

Oliver Temple provides an example into the thinking of many people in East Tennessee. Temple was a slave owner, but he believed that preserving the Union was more important than owning slaves. Many others felt likewise. The Union of the United States was something that their ancestors fought for and they were determined to hold on to at all cost. They believed that the United States would reward their loyalty. They expected United States troops to be sent to free them from the oppression they were suffering. William B. Carter presented a plan to President Lincoln proposing the burning of railroad bridges between Bristol, Tennessee and Bridgeport, Alabama. The Reverend William Blount Carter, a graduate of Princeton University, was a Presbyterian minister from a prominent East Tennessee family of Unionists. His brother, Samuel P. Carter, a graduate of the U.S. Naval Academy, was commander of U.S. forces in southeastern Kentucky early in the war, and another brother James was in command of the 2nd Tennessee Volunteer Infantry, a Union regiment organized in southern Kentucky.

In November 1861, Union sympathizers in East Tennessee carried out a series of guerrilla operations. The plan called for the destruction of nine strategic railroad bridges, to be followed by an invasion of the area by Union Army forces from southeastern Kentucky.

The pro-Union conspirators managed to destroy five of the nine targeted bridges, but the Union Army failed to move and did not invade East Tennessee until 1863, nearly two years after the incident. The destruction of the bridges, which were all quickly rebuilt, had little military impact. However, the sabotage attacks caused a shift in the way the Confederate authorities dealt with East Tennessee's large number of Union sympathizers. Portions of the region were placed under martial law, while dozens of Unionists were arrested and jailed. Several suspected bridge burners were tried and hanged. The actions of the Confederate authorities placed increased pressure on Lincoln to send Union troops into East Tennessee.[45]

In Franklin County, Peter Turney organized a company to fight for the Confederate cause before the June vote was official.

---

[45] Oliver P. Temple, *East Tennessee and the Civil War*. (Cincinnati: The Robert Clark Company 1899) 370–406.

Young men rushed to join the army units forming in their counties and towns. Named Turney's First Tennessee Volunteer Regiment, it included several Grundy County citizens. Company A, which was recruited from Pelham and Altamont in Grundy County, and from Hillsboro in nearby Coffee County, was nicknamed the "Pelham Guard." Turney's 1st would be one of the few Tennessee units to fight the entire war in the eastern theater.[46]

Turney reported to the Confederate War Department that his regiment was organized, but without weapons. They bivouacked on the grounds of Mary Sharp College for three days and as they departed for the Decherd railway station on May 1st their paths were "strun [sic] with flowers from the hands of local women and children."[47]

At the Decherd station politicians made speeches and presented banners. Wives and sweethearts said their goodbyes, and mothers slipped Bibles into their sons' pockets. It was a cheerful, yet somber farewell. In Scottsboro, Alabama, the train

---

[46] Aaron Astor *The Civil War Along the Cumberland Plateau*, (Charleston: The History Press, 2015) 72-73.

[47] Nashville Gazette May 3, 861.

passed an East Tennessee train carrying delegates traveling to the capital in a last-ditch effort to preserve the union.

The troops arrived in Lynchburg, Virginia on May 5th. They were moved to Harper's Ferry Virginia where they were placed under the command of Brig. General Thomas J. "Stonewall" Jackson and took part in the Battle of 1st Manassas, better known as Bull Run. They were to become part of what was known as the Tennessee Brigade of the Army of Northern Virginia and took part in most of the major fighting in the East, including Gettysburg where they were on the left flank of Pickett's Charge on June 3, 18th.

Not all Tennesseans were eager to join the Confederate ranks. Some 31,000 Tennesseans joined the Union Army, more than all the other Confederate states put together. In addition, over 20,000 African Americans from Tennessee later joined the Union Army.

Grundy County

The area that was to become Grundy County had been inhabited by Native American cultures for hundreds of years. It is believed that members of Spaniard Hernando Desoto's expedition were the first Europeans to set foot in what would become Grundy County. Several Native American trails traversed the area, one, the Hollingsworth Trail ran through the Pelham area, near Wonder Cave and ascending the mountain near present day Monteagle. Another trail extended from present day Tracy City to Beersheba Springs and down the mountain to the Collins River area. From the Cumberland Plateau to the Elk River and beyond the district, it was uninhabited except wild beasts, Indians, and a few hunters and trappers.

In 1793, an expedition was sent from the Cumberland settlement to see if it would be practical to build a station at the mouth of the Elk River. Trouble with the Indians in the Nickajack area had caused the settlers to consider this option, or at least search for a way to cross the Cumberland Plateau if a planned attack on the Indians near Nickajack was to be realized.

Late in August a small party under command of Colonel Roberts went out with written instructions to "scour the head waters of the Elk," but with the secret purpose of spying out a route. They camped the first night on the present site of Murfreesboro. From thence, they passed in a southeasterly direction through Coffee County, crossing Barren Fork of Duck River not far from the Old Stone Fort, which still stands near Manchester. The party passed through Greene's Lick and Pond Springs (Hillsboro) toward the head of the Elk...scouring the woods in every direction. They "came upon a fresh Indian trail...soon overtook the enemy...Pursued 1 and killed him." At a ford south of this they crossed Elk River into Franklin County. From there they proceeded over the mountains and camped on the Tennessee River near where South Pittsburg now stands.[48]

The party found no difficulty in crossing the mountain and went on down Battle Creek to the river bottom, and up by Lowry's Island, then nearly opposite to Nickajack, and returned; after walking nearly all night, they were ascending the mountain by sunrise next morning and crossed it that evening on their

---

[48] James Gettys McGready Ramsey, *The Annals of Tennessee to the End of the Eighteenth Century*: (East Tennessee Historical Society, 1967) 477, 608, 616.

homeward march. On the 13th of September, they camped one night on the mountain, and they spent the next night near where Caldwell's Bridge crossed the Elk River in present day Pelham, Tennessee.[49]

In 1794 Tennessee Governor William Blount appointed Major James Orr to lead an expedition to put down hostile activities of a splinter group of the Cherokee originally led by Dragging Canoe. Known as the Nickajack Expedition, they left from Nashville and followed the earlier route and crossed the Elk River near Pelham before crossing the mountain and destroying Running Water and Nickajack, two of the most hostile towns, effectively ending the Cherokee resistance.

Even though Tennessee became a state on June 1, 1796, Middle Tennessee was still part of the Southwest Territory and remained in Cherokee hands. The Cherokee ceded part of what was to become Grundy County in the Third Treaty of Tellico in 1805 and Dearborn's Treaty in 1806. This land included what would become Warren and Franklin Counties in 1807. Later in

---

[49] James Gettys McGready Ramsey, *The Annals of Tennessee to the End of the Eighteenth Century*, (Charlestown: John Russel, 1853) 606-616.

1819 the Cherokee would surrender claims to all land north of the Tennessee River.

With the opening of the new land, settlers swarmed into Middle Tennessee. Historian Frank Owsley has pointed out that agricultural migration and settlement on the southern frontier followed a pattern. They "sought a country as similar as possible to the country in which they lived, in the matter of soil, rainfall, temperature, and appearance."[50] The main reason for selecting a country similar to the one from which they were emigrating was to enable them to continue growing field crops, fruit and vegetables with which they were familiar. Similar soil was important to be able to use the same farming methods and tools as they previously used. Men seldom changed climates because to do so, they would have to change their customs and lifestyles.

Thus, for most, it was a westerly migration, and most of the settlers of Grundy were from North Carolina, South Carolina, and southern Virginia, most arriving through the Cumberland Gap and migrating south. Often neighbors moved together and became neighbors in the new country.

---

[50] Frank Owsley, *Plain Folks of the Old South*, (Louisiana State University Press, Baton Rouge and London. 1949) 52-54.

The earliest settlers in what was to become Grundy County settled along the Elk River in what was then Franklin County. Large tracts of land had been bought by speculators. After the opening of this area, they began to sell off parcels of land to settlers.

Lambert Reed, Solomon Sanders, and Benjamin Nevil were three of the earliest pioneers, Reed in 1808, Sanders in 1812, and Nevil in 1813. Benjamin Holland was known to be an early settler in the area, eventually ending up living between Pelham and Hillsboro, which was then known as Pond Springs. A tombstone near Hillsboro bears the name Tippie Clapper and the date *1781*, which would have put settlers, or at least hunters, in the area before the signing of the Treaty of Tellico.

Attracted to the fertile farmland, settlers flocked into the area. By the 1820s the area was populated enough to support its own church. A. C. Burrows donated to establish a school to serve grades one through eight. As in most rural communities, the one-roomed building was both a church and a school. As early as

1813, Isaac Conger, a Methodist circuit rider, was preaching at the "head of Elk River."[51]

By 1832, Pelham established the first post office in what would become Grundy County. Benjamin Hollingsworth was appointed as the first postmaster. Pelham benefitted from being on the Nashville Stage Road as the Fort Nash (Nashville) to Georgia road was known. In a short time, several businesses sprang up along the line.

Alexander Patton was one of the most prominent men in the 1800's in Pelham Valley. Patton was born in Jefferson County, Tennessee in 1800. While he was still a young boy, his family moved to Franklin County, Tennessee. In 1830, he purchased 200 acres near Pelham, which was at that time a part of Franklin County. In 1831, he married Salina Zora Belle Hollingsworth. In 1835, he gave half an acre to be used for Greenwood School, which would later become Pelham School. The school was located near the site of Old Baptist Cemetery. Patton also donated another half-acre to the Elk River United

---

[51] Isaac Conger, *Diary of Isaac Conger*, 1813. Quoted in *A History of Grundy County Schools*, Janelle Coats Taylor, 69. Website:
http://grundycountyhistory.org/05_Res/Grundy/History_GrundyCounty_Schools7.pdf.

Baptist Church, which was located next to the school. Over the next several years, he added to his holdings and served as a commissioner on several turnpike companies as well as Pelham's postmaster. By 1860, he was the wealthiest man in Grundy County of which Pelham became a part in 1844.

Pelham was in Franklin County until 1836, when it became part of the newly formed Coffee County. It remained in Coffee until Grundy County was formed in 1844. Many residents of the valley were dissatisfied with the new county. In 1847, a petition was signed by 270 valley residents complaining about having to attend court on top of the mountain 'where judge, nor jury, clerk or sheriff nor any other officer can live because of the sterility of the land."[52]

Hubbard's Cove has been in existence since at least 1824, when the name appears on Warren County Plat records. There were several Hubbard's listed on Warren County documents as early as 1806. James Hubbard owned land in the Hickory Creek Valley or Viola Valley, as the area where Hubbard's Cove is located was sometimes identified. The valley is a fertile

---

[52] Chuck Sherrill. *The Heritage of Grundy County, TN*. (Walsworth Publishing Company: USA.) 60.

agricultural land that was well known for fine horses and mules. As with other river valleys, early settlers were attracted to the rich farm land, the abundance of game, and the opportunity to own land.

By 1809, pioneers in Warren County had moved up into the Collins River Valley. The Head of the Collins River Church, which was renamed Philadelphia Baptist in 1858, was established near Savage Gulf near what is known as Wannamaker's Branch.

In 1825, the settlement on the "Cumberland Mountain" petitioned the Head of the Collins River Church to hold meetings on the mountain. The first meeting on the mountain was held near Sterling Savage's place in September 1825, which is likely to be the first church service held on the mountain in what would become Grundy County.[53]

Early settlers, mostly from North Carolina and Virginia, flooded the area looking for land. The Collins River and surrounding farmland attracted pioneers to the lush valley. Settlers began a steady push into the valley.

---

[53] http://www.grundycountyhistory.org/05_Res/Cemetery/HeadofCollinsRiverChurchpfSandra Tate Hereford.

In 1826, William Dugan purchased mountain land on the south side of Little Laurel Creek. He soon began to acquire more land on the mountain nearby. In 1833, Dugan was visited by John and Beersheba Porter Cain. John Cain was a McMinnville resident and a prominent Warren County merchant, land speculator, and part owner of the Rocky River Iron Works.

Mr. and Mrs. Cain rode to the foot of the mountains and stopped at William Dugan's place, possibly to discuss a timber deal. While the men visited, discussing land and a timber deal, Mrs. Cain explored the woods near the homestead. During her walk, she found a distinct path, likely an Indian trail that led up the mountain. As she followed it to the mountaintop, she discovered a chalybeate spring, a mineral spring containing salts of iron that was said to have healing properties. From that time forward, the spring became known as Beersheba Springs.

A few years later, in 1834, Cain purchased the land from Dugan and began to build cabins near the bluff. One of the first tasks must have been to create some type of road to get up and down the mountain. A short time later Dr. Alfred Paine, a McMinnville physician, also built a cabin there. In 1836, George R. Smartt, Dr. Paine's brother-in-law, and William R. Stewart bought the spring and 1,500 acres surrounding it for $1,000. Stewart sold out, and Smartt operated it as a resort for the next fifteen years, building several log cabins, a dining room, and a small hotel of log cabins connected in a long row.

In 1839, Allen White was authorized to open a turnpike beginning at William Dugan's and crossing the mountain at Beersheba Springs. White was also a main investor in the Pelham-Jasper turnpike. The Beersheba turnpike was to have a tollgate two miles south of Beersheba.

Beersheba Springs was incorporated in 1839 and enjoyed a growing reputation as a health resort. Smartt sold the resort to Dr. D.H. Robards of Memphis, Tennessee. Robards was deep in debt by 1854, and he sold the resort to John Armfield. Armfield was a wealthy former slave trader and businessman who was descended from North Carolina Quaker stock. He and Isaac Franklin became wealthy taking slaves from the Atlantic coast, through Nashville, and down the Natchez Trace to the Deep South. The firm of Franklin and Armfield shipped more than 1,000 slaves annually making them one of the largest slave trading operations in the United States.

The journey itself was treacherous, eight weeks on foot marching as many as twenty-five miles a day. Measles and cholera killed many along the way. Franklin wrote that he began sneaking the dead bodies of slaves out of Natchez and tossing them in the many surrounding swamps. The people of Natchez noticed and would no longer allow Franklin to sell slaves within the city limits.[54]

When Armfield retired from the slave trade business in 1845, he began to invest some of his wealth in Tennessee land, and he saw the potential for Beersheba Springs as a resort. He was also anxious to escape the yellow fever that plagued the South during the summers. The solitude of the mountain proved appealing, and Armfield fell in love with the mountains. He built a magnificent wing on the front of the hotel and added several cottages. He brought in French cooks and orchestra players from Louisiana. Under Armfield's tutelage, the resort reached its highpoint.

Armfield purchased one thousand acres of land, the original tavern, dining hall, proprietor's rooms, and row of cabins

---

[54] Betsy Phillips," *The Man We'd Love to Forget*," (Nashville Scene. City Press: Nashville, TN. May 7, 2015) 17-18.

for $37,500. He also bought a nearby residence built from red cedar logs for $1,200. Armfield did some major renovations, hiring Ben Cagle from Irving College as a millwright and foreman, A. T. Mitchell as head carpenter, and T.P. Argo to run the brick kiln, as well as several other local laborers. Legend had it that Armfield brought 100 slaves from Louisiana to work restoring the resort. The tale is largely unfounded as Armfield owned only 32 slaves, according to the 1860 census, and records indicate that he used skilled white laborers and paid by the day with board furnished.[55]

After extensive remodeling, which included work on the road from McMinnville to Altamont, the resort reopened in 1857.[56] Though the railroad made its way to Tracy City less than twenty miles away, the road from Tracy to Altamont was rough and not easily traversed. The road from McMinnville, while longer, very steep and curvy, had a stagecoach to transport guests from the railroad depot.

---

[55] Isabel Howell, *John Armfield of Beersheba Springs*, (Beersheba Springs Historical Society, 2011) 54-55.

To increase the number of residents at his resort, Armfield printed a circular outlining his plans. "My only object in going to the mountain is to preserve health . . . I hope to draw around me a peaceable and respectable society, and thus render it a most agreeable resort." He continued by offering a lot to anyone who was willing to erect a cabin and improve the lot for the nominal price of $1.00. Earlier he had advertised that he planned to keep a "good house of entertainment, but under no circumstances to allow either gambling or the use of spirituous liquors."[57]

In a letter written to the *Memphis Daily Appeal* on July 26, 1861, the writer describes Beersheba Springs as a "charming spot." The writer goes on to explain that as a summer resort it is one of the finest and that "purer atmosphere never blessed this earth." Located two-thousand feet above sea level, the writer boasted that a "mosquito cannot be found here."

The resort has "accommodations for 800 people" and the "rooms nicely fixed." For entertainment there is a "billiard room, ten pin alleys, and riding horses. At night the ball room is open."

---

[56] Information here obtained from *Grundy County* by James L Nicholson, Robert E. Corlew Editor: Memphis State University Press, 1982. The Heritage of Grundy County TN 1844-2004, Walsworth Publishing Co. 2004.

[57] Howell, *John Armfield*, 54-56.

The dining room, under the guidance of Mr. Hukil, who is described as "one of the most accomplished caterers in America," provided meals equal to any "hotel in New Orleans or Memphis."

"Around the hotel are a number of elegant cottages owned by people from Nashville and New Orleans." The spring was located "about two hundred yards from the hotel and accessible by a pleasant road." The writer also noted that the "stone door, waterfalls, and caves" were nearby for those seeking outdoor activities.[58]

In January 1857, Armfield wrote to Bishop James H. Otey, the Episcopal Bishop of Tennessee, asking if a site had been determined for the proposed university. For several years Bishop Leonidas Polk and Bishop Otey had been proposing the creation of a university to educate Southern Episcopal youth. Armfield encouraged both bishops to visit Beersheba before making a final decision for a site.

On July 4, 1857, the founders of what would become the University of the South met at Lookout Mountain.

---

[58] Letter published by the Memphis Daily Appeal, July 31, 1861. Author of letter gives name as Traveler.

Representatives of the nine dioceses finalized plans and selected a committee to research potential sites for the school. The meeting received tremendous attention from the local and national press, and it is through these accounts that Armfield likely became aware of the search. Beersheba met several of the requirements; it was on a mountain, which tempered the humid southern summers and provided a respite from yellow fever. It had natural beauty, springs, and no evils of town life. It is unclear if Beersheba Springs was ever seriously considered; it was not part of the final group when the selection was made. The 1859 meeting of university trustees was held at the Beersheba Springs resort.

Several sites, like Huntsville, Alabama, offered cash and land incentives. Sewanee was the most isolated of those proposed locations. There was no cash consideration, but Samuel Tracy of the Sewanee Mining Company offered to donate 5,000 acres of land, a million feet of pine timber on adjacent lands, free transportation of 20,000 tons of freight on the company railroad which ran through the tract, and 2,000 tons of coal. Additional land was offered by Dr. Wallace Estill, a Virginia native and at that time, a prominent physician in Franklin County, and others.

Though there was only a rough wagon trail up the mountain, the Sewanee site was chosen.[59]

When the Civil War came, Armfield organized and supported a regiment from Grundy and surrounding counties. The 35th Confederate Regiment was organized in the fall of 1861, and Benjamin Hill of McMinnville was elected colonel. Albert C. Hanner, John Armfield's nephew, was chosen as captain. Company "A" was equipped by Armfield and took part in the Battle of Shiloh in April of 1862. During the Shiloh engagement, Hanner was killed. Two other Grundy County soldiers from the 35th Regiment, Lt. Jackson V. Brown and Pvt. Russell L. Brown, the sons of Methodist circuit riding preacher William Sanford Brown of Beersheba Springs, were also wounded there.[60]

Two other towns would gain prominence in Grundy County prior to 1860. By1846, the area at the top of the mountain above Beersheba known as Altamont had grown sufficiently,

---

[59] James Otto Hill, *Sewanee: A Unique Community,* unpublished master's thesis, Middle Tennessee State College, 1952 (Sewanee Archives) Quoted in Arthur Ben Chitty, *Reconstruction at Sewanee: 1857-1872*. Proctor Hall Press: Sewanee, 53-54.

[60] Margaret Brown Coppinger. "Recollections" *Beersheba Springs: A History*. 147.

having approximately 200 people, to have a post office, only the second in the county. Altamont became the county seat of Grundy County in 1846. Being on Higginbotham's Turnpike, the stage route between McMinnville and Jasper proved to be a benefit to the area.

E. Patton, Solomon P. Goodman, William B. Smart, Noah Bass, and John T. Neal, of Bedford County, {were appointed} as Commissioners to locate the County seat of Grundy County. It was their duty to locate the County seat in the center of the county, or as near thereto as possible, having due regard to the locality for its water supply. It was made the duty of the County Court of Grundy County to make an allowance out of any money, unappropriated by law for their services in this regard . . . established Altamont as the County seat of Grundy County. Greek Bawley, John Fultz, Noah Bass, Robert Tate, and Thomas Burrus were appointed as Commissioner to sell the lots in the town according to the plan on which they were laid off and to apply the proceeds to the construction of the necessary public buildings. James Tate, who has already built a house on one of the lots, may dispose of the same and retain the price received. The several courts of the County would be held at the house of Jesse Wooten until suitable arrangements could be made to have them meet in Altamont.[61]

The process of choosing a mayor was changed a short time later as the minutes indicated. *Altamont {was incorporated) under the Mayor - Aldermen form of Charter and government, conferring upon the newly fashioned city all the authority and privileges incidental to municipal types of corporate institutions. The Sheriff, or a Constable, will hold an election within the boundaries of that city on the first Saturday in March, next, for the purpose of electing five Aldermen who would choose one of their number to be Mayor.*[62]

One of the most prominent settlers of Altamont was Adrian Northcutt. Northcutt was born in 1799 in Lee County, Virginia. By 1820, Northcutt had migrated to Warren County, Tennessee and married Sarah Cope. In 1825, he purchased 45 acres of land in Irving College, not far from McMinnville, for ½ cents per acre. It was the beginning of land acquisitions and business dealings that would make him a prosperous landowner. Though not well educated, he was described as having wonderful business ability

---

[61] Grundy County Minutes Books *2. Acts of 184* Chapter 96, Page 147.

[62] *Acts of 1853-54, Chapter 184, Page 254. Grundy County Records.*

and judgment. He was in the forefront of a group of citizens working to establish a new county from land taken from Coffee and Warren Counties.

In 1845, Northcutt was elected to the State House of Representatives. In 1846 he joined the First Tennessee Volunteer Regiment and fought in the Mexican War. He was made captain of Company D, "The Mountain Blues." One of his sons was killed while fighting in Mexico.

Upon returning from Mexico, Northcutt finished his term in the House and was elected to the state Senate in 1849 and again in 1853. In the 1850's he opened the first store in Altamont. His business was a success and by 1854, he owned 9,000 acres of land in Grundy County.

The Civil War proved to be a tragedy for the Northcutt family, as two more of Adrian's sons lost their lives.[62] His son Woodson was killed at the Battle of the Wilderness in Virginia on May 5, 1864, and son S.H. was killed in a skirmish near Manchester. Both were members of Turney's 1st Tennessee Infantry Regiment. A third son, Lawson was captured and spent much of the war in prisoner of war camps. In addition, the

---

[62] http://home.comcast.net/~northcutt/adrian/adrian.htm.

mercantile store operated by Adrian's son Harris Bradford Northcutt was robbed and burned by Union soldiers.

Altamont had the earliest known school on the mountain, the Altamont Academy, which was established February 2, 1848. Jess Wooten, John Myers, William Dangin, (Dugin?) Stephen Griswold, and David Burrows were the trustees. The Academy was closed somewhere around 1884.

In the Antebellum South, on the average, less than 45 percent of the children attended school on a regular basis. Even though 80 percent of the adult population could read and write, though formal education held little sway. There were no public-school systems in the South as there was in the North. Children of wealthy parents were often educated at home with tutors, sent to academies, or to subscription schools.

Most communities had some form of subscription school, such as the Altamont Academy and Greenwood School in Pelham. The families who saw the need for education but were unable to afford the money necessary often worked out a barter system, trading agricultural products for classroom instruction.

Still, education in the South was limited. The South was an agricultural society, and children were needed to plant and harvest crop. Students were limited to going to school for three months after planting and another three months after harvest. Because of the short periods of instruction, instruction was limited to reading, writing, and math.

Most teachers were women, and, in many communities, there was a serious shortage of qualified teachers. In rural areas like Grundy County, the problem was worse. Teachers and students had to travel greater distances to reach schools and most rural schools had only one teacher, who by necessity was forced to teach the first through eighth grades. Often books and other school materials were not available or, at best, outdated. Buying pencils, paper, and other school supplies also placed a burden on families with meager finances. The Civil War increased the education gap between the North and the South.

Though the Northcutts and others were Confederate supporters, several residents of the Altamont area appear to have been pro-Union. Stephen Tipton organized a troop of the Tennessee –Alabama Independent Vidette Cavalry, a Union unit. Several others, Robert Soward Myers, James Fultz, Jesse Fultz, and William Nunley were listed as soldiers in that unit. As in many areas of Tennessee, loyalties were divided, and neighbors were often pitted against neighbors.

In 1832, some 12 years before Grundy became a county, a man by the name of Benjamin Wooten received a large land grant in and around the area that would become Tracy City. He moved his family and carved out a small farm in the area called The Heading.

Wooten's dog chased a groundhog that had been destroying a crop to a hole under a stump. As Wooten's boys tried to dig the groundhog out of the hole, they discovered coal. Thomas Wooten, one of the young boys, explained their discovery many years later:

"Do you see those railroad scales up yonder? Well, right there in that flat we had about two acres that we always put in corn. One fall some ground-hogs began to destroy our crop and we got "after one and treed it under a sourwood not many feet from where the old No. 1 mines are. While scatching and digging after the ground-hog we unearthed a black substance resembling rich dirt which afterwards proved to be coal croppings. But it being away out here in the wild woods did not create any intense excitement for it had not dawned upon the mind of man that

there would ever be a railroad up the mountain to the old Wooten place as it was familiarly called."[63]

There was little demand for coal on the mountain as wood was plentiful to burn. Wooten and his son began digging up the coal in 1845, carrying it on their backs, and selling it to a blacksmith in Pelham.

In 1850, an Irishman named Leslie Kennedy was traveling through the area and spotted Wooten's outcroppings of coal. He took a sample back to Nashville where he attracted the attention of William Bilbo, a Nashville businessman. In 1851, Wooten sold his land to Bilbo who then went to New York City in search of financiers to raise money to develop the coal mines in Tennessee. He sparked the interest of four capitalists and a civil engineer; the leader of the group was a man by the name of Samuel Franklin Tracy.

The men traveled to Tennessee, purchased the land from Bilbo, and then chartered the Sewanee Mining Company. Samuel Tracy was chosen president. The railroad age was just beginning. By 1854 a railroad line reaching from Nashville to Chattanooga

---

[63] Newspaper Article taken from the November 4, 1920 issue of MRS. GRUNDY from the collection of William Ray Turner Olden Times on The Mountain.

had been completed. From near Cowan, Tennessee, the Sewanee Mining Company constructed a branch railroad up the mountain. The line up the mountain was called the "Goat Road" because of the constant curves and bends. Having purchased lands in the Sewanee area that had proved unprofitable, the Sewanee Mining Company extended the railroad line 10 miles to where Thomas Wooten had unearthed coal. The first load of coal from Wooten's discovery was shipped in November 1858. The mines attracted more workers and a town began to grow up. The name chosen was Tracy City, for the president of the Sewanee Mining Company Samuel Tracy.[64]

---

[64] Information here obtained from *Grundy County* by James L Nicholson, Robert E. Corlew Editor: Memphis State University Press, 1982. The Heritage of Grundy County TN 1844-2004, Walsworth Publishing Co. 2004.

Farming

In Middle Tennessee, 6 out of every 10 free head of families in the 1860 census listed themselves as farmers, farm laborers, or overseers.[65] Grundy County was almost a microcosm of Tennessee. Much of Grundy County is atop the Cumberland Plateau and was sparsely populated. The mountain area of this region seldom experienced economic activity beyond subsistence farming. In 1860, many small farms dotted the landscape. Few crops outside of gardens were grown so grazing animals was the primary agricultural occupation.

Opportunity for acquiring land was greater in the South than in the North. Livestock grazing was a major occupation in the South, especially on the Cumberland Plateau where the soil was not especially fertile or deep, but grasses grew well. The first waves of settlers were usually herdsmen and hunters. As long as there were large areas of unsettled lands for cattle and hogs to graze, the herdsmen were fine. In the spring of the year cattle,

---

[65] Stephen Ash, *Middle Tennessee Society Transformed 1860-1870*, p. 13.

[67] Paul E. Sanders, *The Heritage Book of Grundy County*, 164.

sheep, and at times hogs were turned loose into the mountains and allowed to remain there until late fall. Summer heat destroyed much of the grass in the valleys and the mountains contained vast unpopulated areas for animals to roam. Owners visited their herd once a week to take them salt, which prevented them from straying too far. The "Countiss Pen" at the top of the mountain between Pelham and Altamont, named for former owner P. H. Countiss, continued to serve as a grazing area even after the turn of the 20th century.[67]

Grundy County first appears in federal census records in 1850, having just been formed with lands taken from Warren and Coffee counties in 1844. According to published 1850 census data, Grundy County had a population 2,773. It was one of the smallest counties in Tennessee, only Scott and Van Buren counties were smaller. In contrast, neighboring counties of Franklin (13,768) Warren (10,179), Coffee (8,351) and Marion (6,314) far exceeded Grundy in population.

Most of the county's free citizens were white: there were 1,325 white males and 1,197 white females. However, there were 8 free colored males and 7 free colored females. The slave population included 115 males and 121 females. There are 439 family groups appearing on the census (not including slaves), which would mean that the average household included six people.[66]

The agricultural census of 1850 indicates there were approximately 375 farms. Of these, 105 (25%) did not report owning any acreage, probably because they were tenant farmers. This leaves 290 farmers who were landowners—so, about two-thirds of the families in the county lived on their own land.[67]

Much of the land in Grundy County then, as now, was unimproved mountain-side woodland. Of those farmers with "improved" acreage (this term includes pasture lands), the clear majority (82%) owned less than 100 acres. Thirty farms with 100 to 199 improved acres were reported.

Six farmers owned 200 acres or more: Solomon P. Goodman, Thomas Burrows and James Winton with 200 acres each; Alfred Braley and William Dugan with 225 acres each; William Mooney with 250 acres; Adrian Northcutt with 350 acres; and Alexander E. Patton with 730 acres. Patton's plantation,

---

[66]http://grundycountyhistory.org/05_Res/Census/Grundy%20Special%20Census.pdf.

outstripping the others in cultivated land by a sizable margin, was also the most valuable farm, with an estimated value of $10,000. This was twice the value of the next-highest farm, that of Adrian Northcutt. Patton's land was in Pelham, in one of the few large and relatively flat valleys of the mountainous county. Patton owned 38 slaves, while Northcutt managed his acres with only one family of seven slaves. In the language of ante-bellum economics, Patton's acreage and slave labor combined to establish him as both the wealthiest Grundy Countian and the one most able to produce additional wealth.[68]

Both Patton and Northcutt were officers in the Mexican War. Northcutt was a local political leader, founder of the county seat at Altamont, and long-time member of the Tennessee state legislature. Other Grundy Countians held large sections of mountain land, which were not cultivated. Indeed, 28 individuals reported owning more than 1,000 unimproved acres each. Chief among these were Daniel Layne, with 10,400 acres, and Jonathan Tipton, who owned 8,000 acres. Neither Layne nor Tipton were

---

Charles Sherrill's excellent work on census data is used extensively in this section. It can be found at: https://www.grundycountyhistory.org/historical-articles-stories-other-musings/

[68] http://grundycountyhistory.org/05_Res/Census/Grundy%20Special%20Census.pdf.

large crop farmers, each having only 50 acres under cultivation. Their specialty, along with that of many other mountain landowners, was livestock grazing.

Adrian Northcutt owned both mountain and valley lands. He was the only landowner who had large amounts of both types of land. He owned 5,000 unimproved acres in addition to his 350-acre plantation (the second-largest in the county). Northcutt's Cove, which was the center of his holdings, still bears his name. Northcutt was a self-made man, local official, and a member of the state legislature for 10 years. His farm was valued at $5,000, second only to that of Alexander E. Patton, who lived on the other side of the Cumberland Mountain.

Cotton, a main product in more fertile regions of the South, was only produced in small quantities by a handful of farmers, particularly those in the area that later became Tracy City. The largest cotton producer was William Nisbett, with six bales to his credit. Most of the other cotton fanners grew only enough cotton to make one or two bales.

Tobacco was grown in small quantities by more than 30 Grundy County fanners in 1850. The largest producers were John Crabtree and Hamson Tallman, who each reported 300 pounds.

The mountain soil proved too rocky, and even in the valleys, cotton was not a staple crop.

Pork was the meat of preference in this period, probably because it could be cured and kept through the winter with better results than other meats. Twenty-six tanners owned 100 or more swine in 1850. Adrian Northcutt again filled the top slot, joined by Jeremiah Nunley, each owning 250.

A.E. Patton estimated the total value of his livestock at $4550, more than twice the amount estimated by the next wealthiest livestock owner, Alfred Braley. Although not the largest owner of any animal except mules, Patton's holdings were diverse and large in each category. With 730 improved acres, Patton had the space to house and pasture large herds, and his 38 slaves were available to care for them.

Slave ownership was not common among Grundy Countians. Although some surely abstained from the practice on moral grounds, it seems likely that most did not own slaves because they could not afford them, or because their farms were too small to require slave labor. There were 29 households reporting slave ownership, with a total of 236 slaves in the county. This is contrasted with the adjoining flatland counties of

Coffee and Franklin. More than 1,000 slaves lived in Coffee County, and more than 3,000 in Franklin. Even Marion County, mountainous and geographically more similar to Grundy County, had a slave population twice as large as Grundy's. It is interesting to note that the county's largest slaveholder, Alexander Patton, lived on the edge of Grundy County adjoining Coffee County. Of slave-owning households in Grundy County, half occupied farms of at least 100 improved acres. Many of the others owned only a single female slave, probably for household help. Alexander Patton's ownership of 38 slaves was extraordinary for the county: no one else owned more than ten. Thirteen owners of slaves had only one or two slaves in their family, a further reflection on the generally small size of farms and households in Grundy County. The oldest slaves listed were the couple belonging to Jacob Wanamaker [sic], the man aged 70 and the woman 60. Adrian Northcutt also owned a 60-year-old male slave.[69]

---

[69] All information regarding Census Information above was taken directly from *Grundy County Special Census Records 1850-1860* Compiled by Charles A. Sherrill, Nashville: TN, 1986.
http://grundycountyhistory.org/05_Res/Census/Grundy%20Special%20Census.pdf.

An example of slave trading in Grundy County can be found in the 1850 Minute Book:

John Wilder by William G. GUINN, guardian. This day came the complainant by their petition the decree of sale of a Slave named Charlotte as the property of John WILDER miner heir of Nathaniel Wilder, dec'd ... Harris GILLIAM appointed Commissioner to make sale of negro woman named Charlotte in hands of William G. Guinn, the Guardian of John Wilder to whom negro slave has descended ... to make sale of slave in the Town of Pelham ... bidding shall not open under $500....[70]

Another example shows that slaves were not always treated well: *Pelham, Tennessee, August 3, 1857 Mr. J. Jones, Sir: A few days ago I caught George stealing a bag of wheat, besides he is lazy and impudent and besides I feel that I cannot keep him and treat him as I would wish. Therefore, I desire that you would take him. You can have him on the following terms, and no others: "First allow me to whip him, what I think he justly deserves. Second, withdraw the suit and you pay the costs. Third, you pay me from the time you get him until Christmas, and the time he has lost since I have had him. This offer I have made*

This is an excellent source of information about Grundy County in the 1800s.

[70] *Oct. 1850, Grundy Co., Tenn.*
[71] *County minute book I, p174-175.*

thru advice of your friends, and mine, and I believe it to be more than strict conformity to the rules of justice toward you. Feeling confident that you will agree to them, I will wait a few days.

Yours, B. J. Thompson[71]

The Industrial Revolution of the 1790's had not found its way to the backwoods of Grundy County by 1850. According to the Products of Industry schedules, there were only two manufacturing establishments in the county, and both were producing their materials by hand. The enumerators were instructed to list only those establishments where the production was valued at $500 or more. Nimrod B. Sain operated a blacksmith's forge and wood shop, producing wagons and plows. Sain, who is listed as a 33-year-old tanner on the population schedules, employed three men (probably including himself). These men do not appear in Sain's household on the population schedule and may have only been occasional helpers. His listing on the population schedule as a farmer indicates that this business was a part-time occupation. T.J. Wagoner's tannery processed 210 rawhides into 420 sides of leather in the census

---

[71] http://www.sadiesparks.com/jamesjones.htm

year. The population schedules show that Wagoner, too, was a young man (age 29) whose principal occupation was farming. Although the information is stricken out on the industrial schedule, Wagoner apparently made shoes and boots from the leather he tanned. Census enumerator Michael Hoover must have determined that that was a sideline apart from the tannery and not worthy of inclusion on the census.

The population schedules indicate several other establishments, which, it would seem, might have been represented on the industrial census. Whether they were excluded in error, or whether their operations were too small to qualify is uncertain. The Grundy Countians who listed occupations in some area of manufacturing in 1850 were as follows: John Hall, tanner; James Burrell and G. W. Oliver, saddler; Esquire Hunter, miller; 1. Eledge, cooper; William Campbell, cabinet maker; Christian Smith, Henry Moffett and Tyre Smith, wheel wrights; A.E. Moffett, Cornelius Philips and Abram Jones, carpenters; Ambrose Killian, Ballard Wilson, Cleaveland Payne, Jacob Sanders, Wiley Sanders and John Fults, blacksmiths; Anthony Aylor and James Bell, chair makers; John Ware, John Layne, Nathaniel Turner, Joseph Bradshaw, James

Brandon, William Stigall and Thomas & Joshua Warren, wagon makers.

On the eve of the Civil War, the 1860 census indicates a growth in the prosperity of Grundy County. The population had grown about 10 percent to 3,093 (the state population had increased at about the same rate). Grundy's rank in the state increased slightly, as there were now three counties smaller than Grundy (Lawrence, Sequatchie and Union). The number of slaves in the county had increased at about the same rate as the white population, but the number of free blacks (and mulattos, specifically identified for the first time in 1860) had decreased by one, perhaps reflecting the growing intolerance of free blacks, which was endemic in the South. There are 276 farms represented on the agricultural schedules, a decrease of nearly 100 from the 1850 schedules.

Larger farms were more common in 1860, as the number of farmers with 200 or more "improved" acres had doubled to 13. The number of farms containing between 100 and 200 improved acres remained about the same as in 1850, at 32. Alexander Patton continued to have the largest number of acres under cultivation, the same 730-acre figure as he reported in 1850.

A total of 16,902 improved acres were reported, indicating that farmers had cleared and planted nearly 2,000 acres of "new ground" since the 1850 census. Many farmers continued to keep most of their land in pasture and woodland, however. Arthur Long, Jesse Wooten and Jourdin Sanders each had more than 5,000 acres of unimproved land under their control in 1860. Alexander Patton added more than 1,000 unimproved acres to his plantation during the decade, leaving him with a total of 2,873 acres in all when the 1860 census was taken. Patton's farm still had the highest cash valuation in the county, listed at $35,900 in 1860. Next in line were Solomon Goodman ($22,000) and Isaac C. Garretson ($21,700). Patton and Goodman were neighbors in the fertile Pelham valley, while Garretson lived in the first district, in the northwest corner of the county near Viola in Warren County.

Although Adrian Northcutt still retained large acreage, both improved and unimproved, five others had farms with a total cash value greater than his by 1860. Livestock had grown in value, and Alexander Patton's total of $7841 was nearly double the amount he had reported in 1850. Although Patton had more farm animals in 1860, the value of each animal was also greater. Nine farmers reported the value of their livestock at more than

$2000, whereas in the previous decade only Patton and Alfred Braley had passed that mark. Likewise, the 1860 schedules show 35 farms with livestock valued at over $1000, compared with only two in 1850.[72]

---

[72] All information regarding Census Information above was taken directly from *Grundy County Special Census Records 1850-1860* Compiled by Charles A. Sherrill, Nashville: TN, 1986.
http://grundycountyhistory.org/05_Res/Census/Grundy%20Special%20Census.
This is an excellent source of information about Grundy County in the 1800s.

The War

The Confederate Congress met in Montgomery, Alabama, in February 1861 and chose Robert E. Lee commander of the Army of Virginia. Jefferson Davis chose Albert Sidney Johnston to command Confederate Department # 2. Johnston was expected to defend a huge territory stretching from the Appalachian Mountains in the East to the Indian Territory in the West. When Johnston took command of the army there were only 27,000 troops in what would become known as the Army of Tennessee. Many of these were unarmed or improperly armed.[73]

The armies on both sides were made up primarily of volunteers with a few professional soldiers mingled in various units. A large part of the male population of Tennessee would fight in the war. True to its nickname earned in previous wars, the "Volunteer State" provided 187,000 men to the Confederate cause and 51,000 to the Union effort. Most were farmers and common laborers with a few skilled workers and carpenters, as well as several students added to the mix. Officers were usually men of some influence in the local community. Soldiers were often reluctant to obey officers. The only way an officer could acquire influence over the Confederate soldier was by his personal conduct under fire. Officers who were at the forefront of battle and led by example were highly respected.

The North had a greater number of miles of railroads and telegraph lines than the South, thus allowing Union troops to travel more quickly and communicate more efficiently between their headquarters and battle sites. In Tennessee in 1860, there were only 1,200 miles of railroad track, most of which were in East Tennessee.

The Unionists had a superior naval capacity, which included commercial and private vessels in which to transport their troops along interior waterways. Another advantage was the ability to control the open sea and repulse an attack anywhere on the eastern coastline of the Confederacy.

---

[73] Connelly, *Army of the Heartland*..63.

The war placed unprecedented demands on both economies, but the North had a more industrial capacity and agriculture ability. Much of the Southern cropland was in cotton, placing an added burden on the South in attempting to feed their army. Because of the railroad, the North could feed, clothe and arm its troops more easily than the South, even though their supply bases were farther away.

Both sides expected a quick victory. Enlistment periods ran for 3 months to 1 year during the early part of the war, and most expected to be back home before that time. In December of 1861, Lafayette McDowell of White County, Tennessee expressed the sentiments that soldiers on sides were feeling in a letter to his brother. "The officers are in good spirits here, fully believing the North will quit us before long. As we gain every battle. I believe myself that they will let us alone before long . . . . We will run them into Canada if they don't quit."[74]

One of the keys to the Confederate defense in the South was Tennessee. Union strategists developed a three-prong-plan for defeating the South. Devised by Union General-in-Chief Winfield Scott, the Anaconda Plan was designed to stranglehold

---

[74] Amanda McDowell, *Fiddles in the Cumberlands*, 100.

the South. The first part of the plan was a blockade to prevent the South from receiving supplies from European countries. Next, they wanted to capture Richmond, the Confederate capital. The third objective was to control the Mississippi River where much of southern commerce traveled.

As part of this latter objective, Union forces led by Ulysses Grant attacked Fort Henry on the Tennessee River and Fort Donelson, located on the Cumberland River near Dover, Tennessee. Fort Henry poorly situated and almost underwater from the heavy rains, was quickly abandoned by Confederate troops. On February 13, 1862, General Grant began bombarding Fort Donelson from gunboats. Confederate artillery drove the gunboats out of range. Despite their early success, General John B. Floyd, commander of the fort, decided that Fort Donelson was indefensible and decided to break out. The next morning, after heavy fighting, the road to Nashville was open, but the Confederate troops were ordered to withdraw. That night General Floyd and his second in command, General Gideon Pillow, decided to surrender. Col. Nathan Bedford Forrest and his command refused to surrender. That night Forrest took his cavalry as well as others who wished to go along and retreated to

Nashville. With the loss of Forts Henry and Donelson, both Kentucky and western Tennessee were lost to the Confederacy.

Johnston realized that once Fort Donelson fell into Union hands, Nashville could not be defended. The city's defense line that had long been planned had never been completed. Nashvillians had failed to respond to the request for slave labor to build fortifications north of the Cumberland River. Now the river was open to Union advance. Johnston was now worried about being outflanked.

Nashville had served as the supply depot for Johnston's army. With the Union army fast approaching, Colonel Forrest made a valiant effort to save as much food and ammunition as possible. Wagonloads of these supplies were shipped south to be used later, but muddy, washed-out roads and torn-up railroad tracks prevented Forrest from being more successful. As Union troops approached, Nashville was abandoned by the Confederate Army. The heartland lay wide open.

Nathan Bedford Forrest was born in Spring Hill, Tennessee, in 1821. His father died when Bedford, as he was known, was sixteen. He married and moved to Memphis where he became a successful businessman. He became wealthy trading cotton, land,

and slaves. At the outbreak of the Civil War, Forrest volunteered as a private. Governor Isham Harris encouraged Forrest to raise and equip an entire unit at his own expense. He was commissioned lieutenant colonel in June of 1861.

Forrest had no formal military training and only six months of formal education of any kind. However, he seemed to instinctively understand battlefield tactics and the use of mounted troops to wreak havoc on the enemy's rear areas. Forrest earned the nickname "the wizard of the saddle" for his lightening raids, and his rear-area strikes became part of the basis for modern warfare strategies and tactics. He was among the most feared officers of the Civil War—Union major general William Tecumseh Sherman once remarked, "That devil Forrest must be hunted down and killed if it costs ten thousand lives and bankrupts the federal treasury."

On February 24, 1862, the Army of the Ohio led by Don Carlos Buell arrived on the north bank of the Cumberland River and met with Nashville Mayor Richard Cheatham and other citizens, who informed the general of the Confederate withdrawal. Entering the city would be difficult because the Rebels had destroyed the bridges over the river before they left. Buell joined his men in their bivouac overlooking the city, intending to accept the surrender in Nashville the following morning. Governor Harris issued a call for the legislature to assemble at Memphis, and the executive office was moved to that city. In the meantime President Lincoln appointed East Tennessee native Andrew Johnson the Military Governor of Tennessee. He set up offices in the capitol at Nashville. Nashville became the first Confederate state capital to fall to the Union troops.

Buell was a West Point graduate and a veteran of the Mexican War and had been brevetted for bravery three times. He would later earn praise for 'saving" the Union army from defeat at Shiloh. He was described as a brave, intelligent officer, but too cautious and hesitant to commit his troops to battle.

The collapse of the Confederate defense across northern Tennessee and southern Kentucky was unexpected. The secessionists, who had viewed war as something to be fought in Virginia or somewhere else, now had war on their doorsteps. Middle Tennessee was wide open to the invading Union Army.

After leaving Nashville, Johnston led his army to Corinth, Mississippi, a Confederate railroad center. On Sunday April 6, 1862, Johnston's forces met Union forces at Pittsburg Landing on the west bank of the Tennessee River. General Johnston was wounded in the leg during the fighting and died from loss of blood. The first day of fighting resulted in a near stalemate, but the Union Army was reinforced during the night. After a determined fight the following day, Confederate forces, now under the command of P.G.T. Beauregard, withdrew toward Corinth. The battle of Shiloh as it became known was the first great bloody battle of the war with each side having over 10,000 killed, wounded, or captured. After Shiloh, or Pittsburg Landing, as it was known in the South, Governor Harris, who had held

General Johnston while he died, commented that "there is a difference between war on paper and war on the field."[75]

Private Sam Watkins described the horrors of that first major battle:

I had heard and read of battlefields, seen pictures of battlefields, of horses and men, of cannons, and wagons, all jumbled together, while the ground was strewn with dead and dying, and wounded, but I must confess I never realized the 'pomp and circumstance' of this thing called glorious war until I saw this. Men were lying in every conceivable position; the dead lying with their eyes wide open, the wounded begging piteously for help, and some waving their hats and shouting to us to go forward. It all seemed to me a dream; I seemed to be in sort of a haze, when siz, siz, siz, when the minnie balls from the Yankee line began to whistle around our ears.[76]

---

[75] Sam Davis Elliott. *Confederate Governor and United States Senator Isham G. Harris of Tennessee*, (Baton Rouge: LSU Press, 2010) 111.

[76] Sam Watkins, *Company Aytch*. M. Thomas Ingle Ed. (Putman: New York 1999) 27.

Private John Gumm was also surprised by his first experience in battle. "Bombs and Grape Shot fell as thick as hail and minnie balls whising (SIC) round my Years like Bomble (SIC) Bees."[77]

The Shiloh victory not only solidified the Union hold on Middle Tennessee but made Confederate control of West Tennessee extremely tenuous. Memphis, the temporary home of the state government after Nashville's fall, became even more vulnerable as the Union gunboats attacked and seized the river forts to the north. On June 6, after defeating the Confederate fleet protecting the city, Union forces took Memphis, forcing Governor Harris and state officials to flee once again. Tennessee was now under control of the Union Army.

---

[77] Diary of John Gumm. Quoted in *Call Forth the Mighty Men*. Bob Womack. 126.

1862

On April 16, 1862, the Confederate government enacted the Conscription Act because more men were needed to fight the war. After Fort Sumter, there had been many volunteers, but as the war dragged on, men were needed at home to plant crops and take care of their farms. The South was primarily an agriculture area and very dependent on yearly crops. The Confederate Army also suffered a lack of manpower due to battle losses and desertion. Reenlistment time was approaching, and many Confederate soldiers were anxious to go home. The Conscription Act required every white man between the ages of 18-35 to be drafted into the army. The law was greatly resented in most of the South. Soldiers who had been drafted against their will were prone to desertion and slacking their duty. This placed a special burden on Southern Unionists who were often conscripted into an army that directly opposed their beliefs.

Private Sam Watkins explained his view of conscription, which was likely similar to many other soldiers:

Soldiers had enlisted for twelve months only and had faithfully complied with their obligations . . . they had a right to go home. They had done their duty faithfully and well. They wanted to see their families. . . War had become a reality, they tired of it. {From the time the Conscription Act passed} we were simply a machine . . . We cursed Bragg, we cursed the Southern Confederacy, All our pride and valor was gone, we were sick of war and of the Southern Confederacy. . . The war might has well ended then and there.[78]

Resentment also grew out of the belief that the war was becoming "a rich man's war and a poor man's fight." As Parson Brownlow of East Tennessee succinctly put it before the war, "honest yeomanry would be forced to fight for the purse-proud aristocrats of the Cotton States, whose pecuniary abilities {would} enable them to hire substitutes."[79] Although the law made all able-bodied men ages 18 through 35 answerable for three years' service, the draft law permitted draftees to pay a substitute to serve, just as Brownlow had predicted. Further heightening tension was the ratification of the "Twenty Negro Law" in October 1862, which excused one white man from the draft on

---

[78] Sam Watkins, *Company Aytch*, 31-32.

[79] Knoxville Whig, 2 March, 1861. Cited in McKenzie, Robert T. *Lincolnites and Rebels*: Oxford University Press. Oxford and New York, 2006. 69.

every plantation with 20 or more slaves. As historian Bell I. Wiley has pointed out, the "exemption from the draft of a man to oversee twenty or more slaves, generated discontent among the Plain folks."[80]

As the Union Army moved back from West Tennessee after the Battle of Shiloh, foraging parties scoured Middle Tennessee for food. Colonel J.C. Walker of the Thirty-fifth Indiana Regiment was part of a reconnaissance of Middle Tennessee. On June 11, 1862, he was ordered to proceed to Pelham and occupy a gap in the mountain east of there to cut off the retreat of any of the enemy that that might be driven in that direction by General Dumont, then marching toward McMinnville. With some 350 men they marched from Winchester, where he had appointed a provost marshal. As he neared Pelham, he was harassed by bands of guerrillas. They camped at the base of the mountain about 2 ½ miles east of Pelham but were continually harassed by small bands of Confederate Cavalry. After learning that Col. James Starnes, with cavalry forces numbering about 1,600 were in the vicinity, Union forces retreated to Tullahoma, bringing with

---

[80] Bell I. Wiley, *Major Problems in the Civil War and Reconstruction*, Michael Perman, Ed. (Houghton Mifflin Co. Boston-NY 1998), 224.

them several prisoners and horses captured near Pelham.[81] Starnes of the 4th Tennessee Cavalry, one of Forrest's most able commanders, would later be killed at Bobo's Crossroads near Tullahoma screening Braggs retreat to Cowan in 1863.

In June of 1862, Union General James Negley informed General Buell that he had captured a large number of Starnes' men in Hubbard's Cove. Starnes left Hubert's Cove (Hubbard's Cove) and marched to Cowen (Cowan) where they encountered a force of 4,500 under the command of Brigadier-General Negley. Believing he could join forces with Colonels Adams and Davis in Jasper, Starnes retreated to Pelham and then crossed the mountains at Tracy City to beat Negley to Jasper. Upon reaching Tracy City, they learned that Union forces were in possession of Jasper, so they retreated to McMinnville by way of Altamont.

Negley attacked Winchester, crossed the mountains and threatened Chattanooga. Believing he could capture Chattanooga, but not hold on to it, Negley abandoned the idea and retreated through the Sequatchie Valley and back across the mountain to Middle Tennessee. While in Winchester, he assessed fines of prominent Confederates to compensate Unionists who

---

[81] OR, Series I, Vol. X. Pt. 1, pp. 917-918.

had lost property in the absence of Federal rule. It seems likely that he extended the Union control into Grundy County. Negley reported that "the Union people in East Tennessee were wild with joy. They met us by the roads by the hundreds." James B. Fry, chief of staff for Union General D.C. Buell told a slightly different story. Concerning Negley's raid, Fry wrote that it was "outrageous" . . . a scene of pillage and robbery" and that his [Negley] "troops were little more than thieves and robbers."[82] The people of occupied Tennessee would feel the brunt of war for the next three years.

On July 7, 1862, Union Colonel Sydney M. Barness of the Eighth Kentucky infantry, which would later gain fame for scaling Lookout Mountain, wrote to his commander Brigadier-General Negley that his scouts had reported a large concentration of the enemy under Adams, Forrest, and Starnes at Pelham. Pelham, it was reported, was a hotbed for the 'sech' and the roads near there indicate heavy travel by Rebel cavalry.[83]

---

[82] James B. Jones Jr., *Hidden History of the Civil War: Tennessee*, (History Press: Charlestown and London, 2013), 85.

[83] OR, Series 1, Vol. XVI. Part 1, Series 23, p. 102.

Two days later, Nathan Bedford Forrest and his men camped at Altamont. The following day they passed through Beersheba Springs. It has never been questioned as to why Forrest traveled to the mountain before his raid on Murfreesboro. The Murfreesboro Raid has been interpreted as a spontaneous response to the capture and pending execution of several citizens of Woodbury. A letter to Andrew Ewing from Tennessee Governor Isham Harris may offer a different explanation. Harris wrote on July 28, 1862, asking "How did the Herald learn that we were at Altamont and Beersheba planning the Forrest Raid on Murfreesboro."[84] If Harris's letter is to be believed, and there is no reason to doubt it, as Forrest and Harris knew each other before the war and collaborated during several campaigns, Forrest's Raid was not an unplanned raid but a calculated attack on Federal forces in Murfreesboro. Governor Harris urged General Bragg on several occasions to occupy Middle Tennessee, so it is likely he encouraged Forrest, whom Harris described as "brilliant" and a "scourge to the Vandal cutthroats," to attack Murfreesboro.

---

[84] Isham Harris letter to Andrew Ewing, July 28, 1862.

Later in July of 1862, General Braxton Bragg and Maj. General Edmund Kirby Smith met in Chattanooga and planned an invasion of Kentucky. The strategy was to outflank the Union Army under Major General Don Carlos Buell and to galvanize supporters of the Confederate cause in the border state of Kentucky. Promoted brigadier-general July 21, 1862, Forrest was assigned to protect Bragg's left flank during the movement into Kentucky. During what was supposed to be a routine reconnaissance, Forrest was almost captured by Union Troops. "Near Altamont, the Federal forces surrounded Forrest's small forces, but by superior strategy, [he] escaped and made his way back to Sparta."[85] Some records seem to indicate this was on the road between Altamont and Beersheba. It was reported that Forrest had a sharp skirmish with Federal forces in Hubbard's Cove that August.

On August 27th General Buell responded to an inquiry by fellow Union General George H. Thomas, who would later earn the nickname "The Rock of Chickamauga," indicating that the descent down the mountain is easy enough on any of four roads

---

[85] George B. Guild, *4th Tennessee Cavalry Regiment*, (Cool Springs Press, Nashville, 1913), 227.

that diverge from Altamont. He was particularly impressed with the Beersheba road, which he described as an "excellent mountain road." He also mentioned there was an old stage road that went from Pelham to Chattanooga that could be traversed.

Thomas, like Robert E. Lee, was a native of Virginia. He had chosen to remain loyal to the Union despite the displeasure of his family. He was denounced as a traitor to Virginia and many of his former friends shunned him. His family destroyed his old letters and turned his picture around on the wall. Despite being ostracized, he remained faithful to his principles and loyal to his country.

General Henry Boynton in speaking of Thomas said: "of him and him alone can it be truthfully said that he never lost a movement or a battle." [86] General James Steedman praised him most, calling Thomas "the grandest character of the war; the noblest figure of the Great Rebellion; the most accomplished soldier America ever produced."[87]

Buell reminded General Thomas, who was stationed in

---

[86] Benson Bobrick, *Master of War*, p. 334.
[87] Ibid, 334.

McMinnville, to be ready to move at once to Altamont should the Confederate Army move in that direction. He grumbled about the fact that it would be difficult to supply troops should the base be moved to Altamont. "McCook, Crittenden, and Schoepf are at Pelham" and could supply reinforcements if needed. The reference was to generals Alexander McDowell Cook, Albin Schoepf, and Thomas L. Crittenden, whose regiments made up Buell's right flank and who were encamped at Pelham.

Buell visited Pelham in person and was surprised by the lack of preparedness there. Taking a back road to town, he rode through the Union lines without any challenge from Union pickets. Having heard that the area around Pelham was a hotbed of secessionists and that the Confederate cavalry spent a great deal of time in that area, Buell was alarmed that Confederate forces might penetrate the Union line as easily as he had and rout their forces. He had Generals Fry and Schoepf arrested. Though it was only a temporary move, it caused much resentment of Buell.

Expecting Bragg to march through Altamont, Buell ordered General McCook to march from Pelham and occupy Altamont. The road from Pelham to Altamont was rough, steep, and very difficult to ascend. Though he praised the "rich" farmland in Pelham, McCook described Altamont as an "extremely sterile country" with "few farms with any corn." There were several head of cattle running loose on the mountain, turned loose there by farmers in the valleys to graze during the summer. The valley areas were described as more fertile areas and better able to sustain an army. McCook remained there until he had exhausted his food and water. From there he descended the mountain through Hickory Creek Road and camped in Hubbard's Cove.

One reason that Buell was convinced that Confederate forces might move through Altamont was that scouting parties he had sent to the area had uncovered a letter from a Grundy County clerk's son who was in Bragg's infantry, indicating that Confederate forces were on the move and he would be in or near Altamont in a few days. They also received information from Mr. Tipton, a loyal Unionist, and other citizens in Altamont that Confederate forces were expected soon. Buell would soon learn that Confederate troops were in Altamont, but not the bulk of Bragg's army as he had expected.

In August of 1862, General Joe Wheeler commanded the cavalry for Gen. Braxton Bragg. Wheeler was a native of Georgia and a West Point graduate. He reported that on August 28th he was ordered to march toward Altamont and drive in enemy scouts on top of the mountain. With General John A. Wharton, a native of Tennessee who commanded one of Wheeler's divisions, they arrived near Altamont at daylight on the morning of the 30th, drove in the Federal pickets and killed a colonel, captain, and two privates. Their efforts proved to have a more significant impact. Union commander Don Carlos Buell was deceived into thinking General Hardee's entire army corps was attempting to cross the mountains at Altamont. General Buell concentrated his troops at Altamont. After harassing the Union troops until noon, Wheeler retreated and joined Hardee's command as his army marched through the Sequatchie Valley. The path to Kentucky was now wide-open thanks to Buell's concentration of his forces at Altamont.[88]

That same day, Union Brigadier General Thomas J. Wood reported that he sent a small scouting party to Beersheba Springs. They reported that they were told by local citizens that a Rebel force of 15,000 cavalry was encamped on Big Creek, six or seven miles from Altamont. General Wood reported that there were

---

[88] OR, Series 1, Vol.16, pt. 1, p. 893.

several loyal men in Altamont who might provide information on the movement of Rebel troops. Rumors were rampant, but little clear information was available to Union forces in Grundy County.[89]

General Albin Schoepf reported to General George Thomas that he arrived at the foot of the mountain near Pelham as ordered. He complained that there was not enough water there to supply his entire command and that the "country was very poor having been scoured by General Wood" prior to his arrival. He sent foraging parties into the coves and hollows, and they reported that "not a bushel of corn or a ton of hay can be obtained here."[90] In addition to Schoepf's division, McCook's and Crittenden's divisions were also camped at Pelham. Even though the valley was a productive farming area, the foraging of the Confederate and Union armies had stripped the country of valuable resources. Despite the scarcity of food supply, the armies remained in Pelham to protect the bridge crossing the Elk River.

It was also reported at the time that pilfering by Union troops became more prevalent. Some of the Union officers

---

[89] Or, Ser. 1, Vol. 16, pt. II. p.453.

concluded that the rise of stealing was a result of a change in attitude among Union soldiers. Early in the war, their primary motivation had been to preserve the Union. As friends and fellow soldiers were killed in battle, the motives shifted to vengeance. This did not bode well for the people of Grundy County, as they would be continually occupied by one of the two armies for the next 3 years.

By September 24, 1862, notices appeared in the *Winchester Daily Bulletin* requiring all white males over the age of fourteen to report to the provost office to sign an oath of allegiance to the Union. The oath required that citizens swear not to "aid or abet in any way.... the Confederate States of America." Grundy County likely faced similar treatment as adjoining Franklin County.[91]

Buell would later defend his decision before a commission that reviewed his concentration of troops in Altamont. Buell reported that he sent a regiment of infantry to Altamont because he learned that there were several loyal men in the neighborhood of Altamont. From these men he was able to obtain the

---

[90] OR Ser. 1Vol. 16, Part 1. pp. 227-229.
[91] Winchester Daily Bulletin, Winchester TN. September 24, 1862. p. 1.

movements, design, and position of the Confederate Army then currently headquartered in Chattanooga.[92]

Clearly Grundy County was bustling with activity. Lucy Virginia French, a regular at the mountain resort of Beersheba, reported on the happenings there:

"In '62 the Springs had assumed the role of a refuge, where culture and real worth could gain a breathing space . . . The place was really a busy hive. Sewing, knitting, weaving, and cooking went on for the benefit of Lee's army, for boys in Maney's, Hutton's, and Forbes' old regiment, for the sick in hospitals and for dozens of purposes I knew not of. Distinguished men gathered there for a little repose-such men as Judge Bromfield Ridley, R.L. Caruthers, Andrew Ewing, and Gov. Harris." [93]

The presence of Governor Harris in Beersheba was not a secret for long. Asa Faulkner, who described himself as one of the few Union men in the county of Warren, wrote to Andrew Johnson, the military governor of Tennessee, asking for protection for his cotton mill. He reported that "the Southern Cavalry are now in the mountains of this and adjoining counties and are threatening all the Union men. I learned that Gov. Harris

---

[92] OR, Series 1, Vol. 16, pt. 1, p. 168.

and the Hon. A Ewing are at Beersheba Springs, which clearly indicate that the Southern Cavalry are near in force."[94]

Later in 1862, Mrs. French's mood was a little more somber. "Now the iron clamps are down on us again. . . This morning we heard the southerners were coming on every road, and the news made our hearts beat with hope and exultation. . . I saw 15 men flying out the road in groups, some of whom I thought were federals. . . I thought the Southerners are coming." Later some people reported that the Union cavalry had encountered Southerners on the mountain and decided to retire."[95]

Another account describes the perils of enemy occupation. Margaret Davidson Gwyn, who lived at Blue Springs, which later became Viola, Tennessee kept a daily diary. She wrote, "I'm surrounded with danger but thank God he still protects me." The Yankees [are] camped at McMinnville, Hillsboro and even Hubbard's Cove. On June 11, 1862, Margaret wrote, "Went to the store. Heard there were 2,000 Yankees camped last night in Hubbard's Cove and were coming on this way. I didn't stay very

---

[93] Herschel Gower, ed. *Beersheba Diaries* and selections from *Darlingtonia;* (Beersheba Historical Society, 2007), 67-68.

[94] Papers of Andrew Johnson, Vol. 5, pp. 543-544.

[95] War Journal of Lucy Virginia French, entry for August 26, 1862.

long, felt uneasy. Heard later in the evening they were doing a great many bad things above here. Taking people's horses and provisions."[96]

Though the Confederates gained some early successes in their invasion of Kentucky, their progress ended after the Battle of Perryville. Historian James McPherson has argued that the Battle of Perryville had consequences parallel to Antietam as both "threw back the Confederate invasion, forestalled European mediation and recognition of the Confederacy, [and] perhaps prevented a democratic victory in the election of 1862" that would have greatly hampered the war effort for the North.[97]

Bragg withdrew back to Tennessee. The invasion was viewed as a strategic failure, although it had forced the Union forces out of Northern Alabama and most of Middle Tennessee. It would take the Union forces a year to regain the lost ground.

After Bragg's army retreated from Kentucky, they reorganized and were renamed the Army of Tennessee. "Bragg believed that the fertile valleys of the Elk, Duck, and Stone's Rivers would restock his army's diminishing food and storage."[98]

---

[96] Margaret Davidson Gwyn Diary
[97] Drew Gilpin Faust, *The Republic of Suffering*, p. 33.
[98] Thomas Connely, *Autumn of Glory*, 15.

Middle Tennessee had already been foraged by the Union troops, and the area had been designated by the Confederate government in Richmond to supply Robert E. Lee's Army of Virginia.

Bragg had been expected to live off the land, but the foraging by two armies had depleted the countryside. In rural areas like Grundy County foraging parties stripped the farms of crops and livestock, resulting in famine and hardship for the local population. Local government collapsed, law enforcement disappeared, and, in that absence of authority, bandit gangs preyed ruthlessly on inhabitants. Even with a pass from Union commanders, traveling was so dangerous that most rural people simply stayed at home. Schoolhouses and church buildings were unoccupied.

The resources found in Tennessee were vital to the new nation's war-making potential. The fertile land southeast of Nashville provided great quantities of food and animals to sustain the basic needs of the Army of Tennessee. In the mountains themselves, numerous caves provided significant amounts of saltpeter, a common name for the mineral niter, which was a critical ingredient in gunpowder.

Soon after the Confederate government was formed, Samuel D. Morgan, in charge of the Confederate Bureau of Supplies, began a campaign to find sources of saltpeter. He wrote to Arthur S. Colyar, a Franklin County lawyer who played an important role in coal mining in Grundy County, that the "South has no powder, and will mainly depend on Tennessee for it."[99] Providing the few powder mills in the south with enough saltpeter to maintain productions became an important issue for the Confederacy. Several caves in Grundy, Coffee, Van Buren, Warren, and White Counties provided sources of saltpeter.

The South's primary source of gunpowder was Tennessee. The Sycamore Powder Mill was located near Ashland City, Tennessee in Cheatham County. In May of 1861 representatives of the Confederate government entered into an agreement with Nashville businessman William S. Whitman to build a powder mill on "Barren Fork of Duck River, at the lower end of Stone Fort, about a mile from Manchester."[100]

By February 1862, the mill had reportedly produced 125,700 pounds of black powder. In March of that same year, Union

---

[99]http://infosys.murraystate.edu/KWesler/Symposium%20OVHA%20Volume%201 7/V17_p063072.pdf.

forces occupied much of Middle Tennessee. Lieut. Col. H.W. Burdsel was ordered to march from Tullahoma to Manchester. Passing himself off in the dark as a Confederate officer, Burdsel captured four prisoners, but found the cabins that served as guardhouses around the powder mill deserted. He emptied the powder found in the works and set fire to five buildings, burning machinery, houses, and materials.[101] Production was never resumed, and the scarcity of powder continued to be an issue for the South.

Similarly, mines near Ducktown, Tennessee, produced 90 percent of the Confederacy's copper, raw material for percussion caps and artillery projectiles. In strategic terms, the region served as a buffer protecting the Confederacy's industrial and agricultural heartland in Alabama and Georgia. Taken together, the multiple mountain ranges and the Tennessee River acted as a series of physical barriers that could delay, if not deny, Union access to the Confederacy's interior for years.

---

[100] Ibid
[101] Ohio Valley Historical Archaeology, Volume 17. 2002. p. 65.

For the Union, too, this theater of war was critical to national success. Because southeastern Tennessee provided food, fodder, and animals to sustain the Army of Tennessee, the Union needed to deny it to the Confederacy. Because the mineral resources of the southern mountains contributed mightily to the Confederate war effort, those resources had to be snatched from Richmond's grasp as soon as possible. If the heartland of the Confederacy was ever to be conquered, the natural defense of the Tennessee River and the Appalachian Mountains had to be overcome.

This reason loomed large in the thinking of the Union. Thousands of citizens in eastern Tennessee, northern Georgia, and northeastern Alabama remained loyal to the Union and suffered persecution for that loyalty. Thus, the North desired to regain control of the region to reduce the Confederacy's war-making capacity, to facilitate further conquests, and to free masses of people believed to be held against their will.

In the fall of 1862, trying to protect the Heartland from more Union foraging, Bragg moved his army to Murfreesboro, which offered little in the way of a natural defensive position. Several of Bragg's top officers argued against making a stand there. Worse still was that Murfreesboro was only 30 miles from the Union base of operation in Nashville. The Union Army would have little trouble resupplying their troops should they attack Murfreesboro. Bragg's supply base was nearly 100 miles away, across the rugged Cumberland Mountains to his base in Chattanooga, TN.

General Buell's loyalties were called into question due to his strict policy of noninterference with the Southern population. He brought charges against subordinates who looted, which did not always sit well with those under his command. His position was further weakened by the fact that he owned slaves, who had been inherited from his wife's family. After Bragg's invasion of Kentucky and Buell's failure to destroy the Confederate Army, Buell was replaced. His conciliatory policy toward southern civilians was also replaced with harsher tactics. Armed combatants he expected to be treated as enemies, but civilians he believed should be treated as United States citizens. He assumed that most white southerners were loyal to the Union and would remain so if not hardened by the occupying forces. Buell believed a limited war would serve the purpose better than total war that would be practiced by Sherman and others. As a result,

Buell was criticized for being a southern sympathizer. After Buell's dismissal, life became much more severe for occupied areas of Tennessee including Grundy County.[102]

On the 26th of December 1862, hard drinking and hot-tempered General W. S. Rosecrans, who had replaced General Buell in the command of the Army of the Cumberland, began to move against the Confederate forces at Murfreesboro. Rosecrans was a complex personality. He was taciturn, yet volatile; extremely religious, yet admittedly a man who still "curses and damn when I'm indignant, but I never blaspheme the name of God."[103]

Rosecrans left Nashville on December 26 with about 45,000 men. He found Bragg's army on December 29 and went into camp that night, within hearing distance of the rebels. At dawn on the 31st, Bragg's men attacked the Union right flank and drove the Union line back to the Nashville Pike by 10:00 A.M. The Union line held there and then slowly advanced. Rain, sleet, and fog combined with spirited resistance from Confederate cavalry

---

[102] Stephen D. Engle, *Don Carlos Buell: Most Promising of All*, (The University of North Carolina Press, 2014), 137-151.

[103] Fredrick D. Williams, Ed. *The Wild Life of the Army: Civil War Letters of James A. Garfield*, (Michigan State University Press, 1964), 227.

slowed the Federal advance to recapture the ground they had lost.

By the evening of December 30, 1862, the armies faced each other in the fields and forests, west and south of Murfreesboro. At every pause in the action, far away could be heard the military bands of each army. Finally, one of them struck up 'Home Sweet Home.' As if by common consent, all other airs ceased, and the bands of both armies, as far as the ear could reach, joined in the refrain.[104]

At dawn on December 31, 1862, J. P. McCown's Rebel Division, with General Patrick Cleburne's men in support, stormed across the frosted fields to attack the Federal right flank. The ground itself helped stave off disaster for the Union forces. The rocky ground and cedar forests blunted the Confederate assault, and Rebel units began to come apart. Confederate artillery struggled to keep pace with the infantry. The Army of the Cumberland's right flank was shattered beyond repair, but reinforcements had saved the day for the Federals.

---

[104] Sam Seay, *1st. TN Infantry*. Stones River Battlefield National Park Service.

Sam Watkins of the First Tennessee Infantry, CS was amazed at the bloodshed:

"I cannot remember now of ever seeing more dead men and horses and captured cannon all jumbled together, than that scene of blood and carnage ... on the (Wilkinson) ... Turnpike; the ground was literally covered with blue coats dead."[105]

The Battle of Stone's River was one of the bloodiest of the war. More than 3,000 men lay dead on the field. Nearly 16,000 more were wounded. Some of these spent as much as seven agonizing days on the battlefield before help could reach them. The two armies together sustained nearly 24,000 casualties, almost one-third of the 81,000 men engaged. Sam Watkins, who was in the heat of the battle, reported that on the final assaults "Rebels were falling like leaves of autumn in a hurricane."[106]

On January 1, 1863, while the fighting at Stone's River raged, Abraham Lincoln's Emancipation Proclamation went into effect. The Proclamation freed all the slaves in the states that were in rebellion. The Proclamation outraged Southern opinion. Fears of freed slaves and race wars alarmed even potential Union

---

[105] Sam Watkins, *Company Aythc*, p.59.

supporters. The conciliatory policy, evident in the early part of the war, was replaced by the hard hand of war.[107]

Andrew Lytle correctly pointed out that the "strategy of the North changed from the eighteenth-century tactics of restricted war to what we now call total war, war on the entire population, with the immediate aim of destroying the enemy's means of conducting hostilities. The Civil War was the first world war.[108]

---

[106] Sam Watkins. *Company Aytch*, P. 58-59.

[107] Mark Grimsley. *The Hard Hand of War: Union Military Policy toward Southern Civilians 1861-1865*, (Cambridge University Press: Cambridge and New York, 1995), 92-93.

[108] Andrew Lytle, *From Eden to Babylon: The Social and Political Essays of Andrew Nelson Lytle*, M.E. Bradford Editor, (Washington D.C.: Regnery Gateway, 1990), 132, 147.

1863

Despite the battle being a stalemate, Bragg left Murfreesboro on January 4th or 5th, and retreated to Shelbyville and Tullahoma, Tennessee, on the main line of the Nashville and Chattanooga Railroad. The railroad line gave Bragg a line of communication with Chattanooga, Atlanta, and Richmond. The Confederate line extended some one hundred miles from Shelbyville to McMinnville.

For the next six months following the battle of Stone's River, Bragg and Rosecrans uneasily faced each other in Middle Tennessee. Despite repeated urgings from Washington, Rosecrans refused to move from Murfreesboro until he felt his army was ready. Meanwhile he strengthened his cavalry, so it could compete with the likes of Confederates Nathan Bedford Forrest, John Hunt Morgan and Joseph Wheeler. To do so, he created what was to become known as Col. John Wilder's Lightning Brigade, which featured mounted infantry armed with Spencer repeating rifles.

The Spencer repeating rifle has been described as the most advanced infantry weapon in the world of its times. It was patented in 1860 by Christian Spencer, a machinist who worked in Hartford, Connecticut for Sharps, but he had developed the Spencer on his own time.

It was the world's first practical repeating rifle and fired a .52 caliber cartridge. It was a revolutionary idea: mount infantry on horses, which would enable them to move rapidly. On top of that, arm them with the 7-shot Spencer repeating rifle, and use them to attack the flank of the enemy. They would ride ahead of the main force, dismount, and attack the enemy with the force of a much larger body of traditionally armed infantry.

The repeating rifle had a great advantage over the muzzle-loading rifles such as the Enfield and Springfield, not only in the rapidity of fire, but also in the ability of the shooter to aim each shot. In a normal battle situation, the muzzleloaders were fired in an aimed manner only the first few shots; thereafter, it was usually a case of hurried fire after frantic loading. A trained soldier could get off two or three shots a minute with a muzzleloader until the barrel fouled with lead deposit. With the Spencer, the soldier could fire 20 to 30 times a minute when necessary, taking advantage of the cartridge box which held 10 preloaded magazines.

Rosecrans gave Wilder the approval to comb the surrounding countryside for horses. Wilder also contracted with Christian Spencer for the delivery of 1,400 repeating rifles and arranged with his bank so that the members of his brigade would pay the purchase price of thirty-five dollars per rifle in installments out of their monthly pay. Later, the government assumed this debt. At Hoovers Gap, Tennessee, Confederate General Patrick Cleburne remarked that the Union Army produced "continual fire" which he could not match.[108] Cleburne, a native of Ireland, had established a reputation as a superb combat officer, and he would later be killed in a gallant charge at the Battle of Franklin.

Of more immediate concern, his two top generals, Leonidas Polk and William Hardee, had lost faith in Bragg's ability to command. In late January 1863, President Jefferson Davis sent General Joseph E. Johnston to investigate the Army of

---

[108] https://www.murfreesboropost.com/community/deception-firepower-made-hoover-s-gap-aneasy-victory/article_42094593-f5e0-5b0b-8a3b-ed4ba798f908.html.

Tennessee's increasing displeasure with Bragg. Bragg was nearby in Winchester, visiting with his wife who was ill when Johnston arrived. Johnston was thus placed in an awkward situation, as he was in line to replace Bragg. If he gave a negative report about Bragg, it would appear that he was being critical of Bragg in order to assume command. Seeking to avoid the appearance of Machiavellian intrigue, Johnston left, and Bragg remained in command. Johnston returned in March to take over command, but Bragg was in poor health and Johnston stayed until May before once again leaving with Bragg still in command.

British Army officer Lieutenant Colonel James Arthur Fremantle, who spent 3 months with the Confederate Army in 1863 as an observer, noted in his diary that Bragg was "very thin. He stoops, and has a sickly, cadaverous, haggard appearance."[109]

Bragg had divided the Army of Tennessee into three corps, and the 1st Corp was placed under General Leonidas Pope, a native of Raleigh, North Carolina. Leonidas Polk was born in Raleigh, North Carolina, April 10, 1806. He had graduated from West Point at the age of 21, in 1827, but chose to enter the

---

[109] James Arthur Fremantle. Fremantle Diaryhttp://docsouth.unc.edu/imls/Fremantle/fremantle.html.

ministry instead of the military. His ministry would evolve from missionary work to Bishop of Louisiana, and to Tennessee as a founding father of the University of the South at Sewanee. Polk had a summer home in the Beersheba Springs area in Grundy County and planned to live on the Cumberland Plateau while the school was being built. The construction of the future Episcopal University was interrupted by Tennessee's secession from the Union and its entrance into the War Between the States.

In 1861, Polk entered the Confederate army. His leadership in the church and friendship with Jefferson Davis soon earned him a promotion to major general. Polk's critics accused him of being arrogant and unaccustomed to taking orders from anyone but God. He would be criticized for missing opportunities for victory, for attacking when he should have been defending, and for being too late or not there at all. Historians have judged Polk as a mediocre, if not an ineffectual, commander.

Tall, soldierly, good-looking, and gentlemanly, Polk had little military experience and may have lacked ability, but his men believed him to be a competent and effective leader. While Bragg was harsh often cruel to his men and his subordinates, General Polk, following his Christian beliefs, was a great motivator who showed compassion for the men under his command. He was considerate of his men, fearless in battle, dignified, imposing, and loved by his staff.[110] According to author Glenn Robbins, "Throughout his colorful military career, Polk remained extremely popular with his fellow officers and enlisted ranks."[111] He was known as the "Fighting Bishop."

Tragically, he was killed by a cannonball, June 14, 1864, on Pine Mountain, near Marietta, Georgia. His death ended a life of service and dedication that is best summed up by author Cheryl White: "There can be no question that his presence inspired a general feeling of wellbeing for the troops with him or near him."[112] Polk's death was mourned by those under his command. His presence in the Cumberland Mountains was short lived, but his legacy still looms large 150 years later.

Lieutenant General William Joseph Hardee was given command of the Second Corp. Born in Savannah, Georgia,

---

[110] Joseph H. Parks, *General Leonidas Polk, CSA: The Fighting Bishop*.(Baton Rough: LSU Press, 1961), 43-54.

[111] Glenn Robbins, *The Bishop of the Old South: The Ministry and Civil War Legacy of Leonidas Polk*, (Macon: Mercer University Press, 2006), 183.

[112] Cheryl White, Confederate General Leonidas Polk: Louisiana's Fighting Bishop, (Charleston: The History Press), 64-70.

October 10, 1815, he had served as commander of the U. S. Military Academy at West Point. Hardee had written what was 'the' textbook on military strategies, *Rifle and Light Infantry Tactics*, which was required reading for officers in both the Union and Confederate armies during the Civil War. In January 1861, he joined the Confederate forces, in which he was appointed a brigadier general in June. Known as "Old Reliable," he and Bragg often clashed.

Edmund Kirby Smith commanded the 3rd Corp. Kirby-Smith was a Florida native and a West Point graduate. In 1861, he resigned from the U.S. Army and joined the Confederacy. Early in 1862, he was dispatched to command in East Tennessee.

Cooperating with Braxton Bragg in the invasion of Kentucky, he scored a victory at Richmond and was soon named to the newly created grade of lieutenant general. After the Kentucky invasion and the retreat at Murfreesboro, he too had little faith in Braxton Bragg. In 1863 he was transferred to the Trans-Mississippi West, where he served for the balance of the war.

Meanwhile, Bragg struggled to obtain subsistence for his army while he waited for Rosecrans to attack him. Ironically, though the Confederates were stationed for the protection of agricultural supplies of the South moving by rail through Chattanooga, they were close to starving while large portions of those agricultural supplies were shipped east to General Robert E. Lee's Army of Northern Virginia.[113] As Private Watkins explained, "Rations with us were always short. No extra rations were ever allowed to the Negroes that were with us as servants, no coffee, whiskey, or tobacco were ever issued to the troops. . . We were starved skeletons; naked and ragged rebels."[114]

On June 23, 1863, it started to rain, and it would rain steadily and often hard for the next eleven days. Despite the weather, Rosecrans decided to advance on June 24. He did so with speed and skill. Sending forces under General Thomas Crittenden on diversionary movements to the east toward McMinnville, and elements of the Reserve Corps under Major General Gordon Granger moved due west from Murfreesboro to

---

[113] Beck, A.M. Spencer's Repeaters in the Civil War. http://milpas.cc/rifles/ZFiles/United%20States%20Rifles/SPENCER%20CIVIL%20WAR%20C ARBINE/SPENCER%20CIVIL%20WAR%20CARBINE.htm.
[114] Sam Watkins. *Company Aytch*, p. 33.

Triune, to begin an elaborate feint. This was designed to play into Bragg's assumption that the main attack would come on his left flank in the direction of Shelbyville. Rosecrans sent his main force straight ahead through Liberty, Hoover's, and Bell Buckle Gaps toward Manchester, Tennessee.

The Union Army was advancing in rough country with several easily defended passes to overcome, but a swift-moving advance by Colonel John Wilder's mounted infantry brigade, armed with the Spencer rapid fire carbines, broke through Confederate forces at Hoover's Gap. Rosecrans was now on Confederate General William Hardee's Corps flank, with a road open to his rear. Bragg had no choice but to fall back on his supply base at Tullahoma and there prepared to defend against an attack by the Federal forces. On June 25th Bragg retreated from Shelbyville to Tullahoma. Shelbyville was a hotbed of Union sentiment and Bragg feared he would be cut off from his supply depot in Chattanooga.

Wilder's forces captured Manchester on June 28th, meeting little resistance. They destroyed the trestle works on the McMinnville branch of the railroad and headed toward Hillsboro. Confederate Colonel John Dibrell, whose cavalry company had been in Grundy County, rode to Hillsboro where they learned the objective of Wilder's movements was the railroad at Decherd. Dibrell rushed his 8th Tennessee regiment to Decherd to reinforce the small garrison stationed there. Their arrival would limit the damage Wilder would do.

Having reached Manchester on June 27, however, Rosecrans again deceived Bragg by moving southeast instead of southwest and moved around Bragg's right flank. This movement now threatened the railroad that was Bragg's line of supply. Heavy rains made the Elk too deep to ford, and there were only 3 bridges in the vicinity that would suffice for Bragg and his army to cross. One was south of Tullahoma, one near Estill Springs, and the other at Pelham. Bragg preferred to use the bridge at Pelham or Estill Springs to protect the railway line that went through the tunnel at Sewanee.

When Wilder's forces arrived at the Elk River near Decherd, they found that the "incessant rains" of the last few days had swollen the stream until it was impossible to swim or ford. The bridge was heavily protected by Confederate forces. They learned from a Union sympathizer that there was a bridge at Pelham, 6 miles to the east on the Elk River.

On June 29th Wilder's force overran the small force of Confederate pickets guarding the bridge at Pelham. Bragg soon learned the bridge and the area around Pelham was in Union hands. After setting up a base in Pelham, the Union cavalry attacked the railroad depot at Decherd, tearing up tracks and cutting off Bragg's communication with Chattanooga. Colonel Wilder described the events:

"On leaving the direct road to Decherd, and going in the direction of Pelham, we were compelled to ford streams that swam our smallest horses and compelled us to carry our howitzers' ammunition on the men's shoulders across the streams. When near Pelham, we learned that a party of rebels were at the bridge, with the intention of destroying it on our approach. I immediately ordered the advance, under Lieutenant-Colonel Kitchell, Ninety-eighth Illinois, (Kitchell would be cited for bravery and gallant conduct on several occasions) and about 30 scouts of the different regiments, to go forward on a run and prevent the destruction of the bridge. They dashed forward, not only saving the

bridge, but taking 2 of the party prisoners, and capturing a drove of 78 mules, which were sent back to Hillsborough in charge of a company. We soon reached the South Fork of Elk River and found the water deep enough to swim our tallest horses. The stream, though rapid, could by crossing diagonally, be swum; and, by tearing down an old mill, we made a raft that, by being towed with our picket ropes, floated our two mountain howitzers over. The crossing occupied about three hours. We immediately moved forward toward Decherd, half fording and half swimming another stream on the way. We reached the railroad at 8 o'clock in the evening, and immediately attacked the garrison of about 80 men, who, protected by a stockade and the railroad cut, made a pretty good resistance. We soon dislodged them, however, when they took a position in a deep ravine, with timber in it, completely protecting them, while our men had to approach over a bare hill to attack them, exposing themselves to sharp fire at 60 yards' range. I ordered up our howitzers, and a couple of rounds of canister silenced them and drove them out. We immediately commenced destroying the railroad track and water-tanks on the Nashville and Chattanooga Railroad, and blowing up the trestle-work on the branch road to Winchester. The railroad depot was well filled with commissary stores, which we burned. We also destroyed the telegraph instruments. A large force was by this time approaching from the north side, and, having destroyed about 300 yards of track, we left, after skirmishing with their advance guard and capturing some 4 or 5 prisoners, who, on being questioned separately, stated that six regiments of infantry were about to attack us. Believing that I would have but little chance of success in a fight with them, on account of the darkness and our total ignorance of the ground, we moved off in the direction of Pelham, and, after going about 6 miles, went off the road into the woods at 2 o'clock, and bivouacked without fires until daylight."

One of Wilder's men, Benjamin Magee of the 72nd Indiana, described his company's uncomfortable night in the mountains. [We] *simply stopped in the bushes and lay down to sleep, holding our horses' bridles in our hands. We had put in a hard day's work in the rain, and our beds were on the mountain side on the sharpest of rocks. The mountain was so steep that we had to get our feet against the trees or rocks to keep from slipping down.*[115]

Wilder wrote in his official report:

When we started again up the Cumberland Mountains, on the Brakefield Point road, I determined to break the road, if possible, below Cowan. When partly up the mountain we could plainly see a

---

[115] Benjamin Magee, *History of the 72nd Regiment*, p. 134. Quoted in Blue Lightening, 53.

https://archive.org/stream/historyof72dindi00mcge/historyof72dindi00mcge_djvu.txt.

considerable force of infantry and cavalry near Decherd. We moved forward to the Southern University, and there destroyed the Tracy City Railroad track. From there I sent a detachment of 450 men, under Colonel Funkhouser, of the Ninety-eighth Illinois, to destroy the railroad at Tantalon, and went forward myself in the direction of Anderson, intending to strike the railroad at that place. Colonel Funkhouser reported to me that three railroad trains lay at Tantalon, loaded with troops, and my scouts reported two more trains at Anderson. Both places being approachable only by a bridle-path, I deemed it impossible to accomplish anything further; besides, the picket force left at the railroad, near the university, were driven in by cavalry, who preceded a railroad train loaded with infantry. They were now on my track and in our rear. I collected my force and determined to extricate them. Leaving a rear guard to skirmish with and draw them down the mountain, I started on the road toward Chattanooga. When about 8 miles from the university, during a tremendous rain, which obliterated our trail, I moved the entire command from the road about 2 miles eastward into the woods, leaving the rear guard to draw them forward down the mountain, which they did, and then escaped through the woods and joined us, some not coming up until next morning. As soon as the rebel column had passed us, we struck through the mountains, without guides, in the direction of Pelham, and came out at the place we intended to strike, and reached the foot of the mountain, at Gilham's Cove, over a very rocky and steep road.

We bivouacked at 10 p.m., and next morning at daylight started for Manchester, just getting ahead of Forrest, who, with nine regiments of cavalry and two pieces of artillery, aimed to intercept us at Pelham[116].

The control of the bridge across Elk River in Pelham has never been recognized by historians as a major target, but it is obvious that Union control of this bridge unnerved General Bragg who feared he would be outflanked. Benjamin Magee of the 72nd Indiana realized the importance. He wrote:

It continued to rain. Many horses gave out and were killed, while others were left to fall into the hands of the rebels. The constant rain had swollen the Elk River out of its banks and the bridge at Pelham was our only chance of crossing; and should the enemy destroy that, our chances of escape were slim. Just before going down the mountain a detail from Company I, Lieut. Vance in command was pushed forward to the bridge and arrived in time to drive off a rebel force that had just reached the bridge. Our boys tore up the floor of the bridge, carried the boards to our side, built breastworks of them and held the fort until morning. We

---

[116] Richard A. Baumgartner, *Blue Lightening: Wilder's Mounted Infantry Brigade in the Battle of Chickamauga,* (Huntington, W. Va.: Blue Acorn Press, 1997), 60-65.

remember the names of the Munson, Wyatt and Allen, of Company I, who took part in this brave and important work. The brigade went into camp immediately on coming down from the mountain, and for the first time since leaving Manchester we had a chance to make coffee.

On the morning of the 30th, we succeeded in getting across the bridge with, but one man wounded, although Wheeler's rebel cavalry were pressing us hard. In actual damage done to the enemy this expedition was a failure, but in unifying the brigade and giving each man confidence in himself and his officers, it was a grand success. The rebels had hitherto had it all their own way in raiding railroads; this expedition demonstrated that we were just as competent to raid rebel railroads as rebels were to raid Union railroads. This raid had a very demoralizing effect on Gen. Bragg, and he began to evacuate Tullahoma in two hours after he heard the report of our guns at Decherd, thinking he had been flanked by the whore army. We failed to say it rained all day the 30th.

Wilder continued his report.

We reached Manchester at noon, having been in the saddle or fighting about twenty hours out of each twenty-four for eleven days, and all the time drenched with rain, our men half-starved and our horses almost entirely without forage, yet our officers and men seemed willing and cheerful, and are now only anxious for another expedition, if by such they can accomplish any good. We did not lose a single man in our expedition to the rear of Tullahoma. If our course had not been impeded by the streams flooded beyond all precedent, we must have captured one or two railroad trains, one of them having General Buckner and staff on board; we should have had ample time to have thoroughly torn up the railroad in daylight at several points, whilst on account of the darkness we were compelled to follow the main roads, and the time lost in going via Pelham enabled the rebels to throw a large force in pursuit of us.

I am, very respectfully,

J. T. WILDER, Colonel Seventeenth Indiana Infantry, Commanding Brigade.

Forrest left Decherd with his command, determined to intercept Wilder at Pelham. It was raining very hard, and Forrest and his escort galloped ahead of the rest of the command. Forrest was very familiar with Pelham, having camped there at various times over the past two years. He also had a loyal network of civilians who fed him information about enemy movement. Turning a bend in the road near the center of town, he encountered a company of the enemy on the road to Manchester.

Both were dressed in raincoats that gave no hint of their colors. Sensing he was outnumbered and at a distinct disadvantage, Forrest rode confidently up to the officer riding in front of the command and asked, "What command?"

The officer responded that he was part of Wilder's command. Forrest replied that he was part of another Union command scouting the area. The two officers saluted and rode on.

Forrest, thinking that the rest of his command was close behind, prepared to block Wilder's retreat. Before he could do this, he discovered the main column of Wilder's command a short distance down the road. By the time Forrest's command arrived, Wilder's men were past Hart's Tan Yard, two miles north of Pelham, and all Forrest and his men could do was to threaten Wilder's rear guard as they rode into Union-held territory.[117]

---

[117] Andrew Nelson Lytle, Bedford Forrest and His Critter Company. G.P. Putnam's Sons: New York, 1931.185.

Bragg's men dug in at Tullahoma, preparing fortifications for the anticipated battle, but Bragg wavered between making a stand and retreating. He gave a series of conflicting orders, cutting timber to make a defensive position, and then suggesting that entrenchment demoralized soldiers and that he would go on the offensive and attack Rosecrans.

Bragg continued to be in ill health and to squabble with his subordinate officers and the government in Richmond. Rumors that he had lost the confidence of his command haunted Bragg, who conferred with his officers as to the truth of the rumor. Rather than resolving the army's internal problems, it only added to the confusion. General Hardee pointed out that Tullahoma was "vulnerable to both direct and flank attack with no advantages to outweigh its faults."[118]

---

[118] Grady McWhiney and Judith Lee Hallock, *Braxton Bragg and the Confederate Defeat, Vol. 2*. p. 13.

On June 29, 1863, Bragg met with Hardee and Polk to discuss whether to make a stand in Tullahoma. Polk was vehemently against it. He advised immediate retreat. Hardee proposed a wait and see attitude, and it appears that was what Bragg decided to do.

But by early in the morning of June 30th, Bragg had decided to abandon Tullahoma. That morning, Forrest's cavalry, on the roads between Hillsboro and Pelham and near Manchester, had been forced to retreat because of the Union onslaught. Bragg ordered immediate retreat. By midday he had crossed the Elk River and ordered the bridges destroyed. Once again, he was faced with indecision. "Shall we fight at the Elk, or take post at foot of mountain at Cowan?" Bragg asked his commanders after they had crossed the Elk River. Both Polk and Hardee advised retreat to Cowan, with Hardee strongly suggesting they fight there. "Let us fight at the mountain," Hardee wrote to Polk.[119] Cowan was at the foot of the mountain on the lower end of the Cumberland Plateau and was a natural defensive position. The mountains themselves would have prevented any flanking action by Union troops. Near Cowan, the Nashville & Chattanooga

---

[119] Hardee to Polk, July 1, 1863. Official Records.

Railroad passed through a long tunnel before coming out near Sherwood. Compounding the loss of Tennessee, Bragg failed to order the destruction of the tunnel. It proved to be a vital supply line for the Union Army for the remainder of the war.

Hardee would later write to Polk that he hated to see Bragg in this "enfeebled" state of health. He expressed his doubt to Polk of Bragg's mental and physical condition and his ability to make decisions should it come to a fight.

Bragg's right flank was threatened, and he feared his access to Chattanooga and the supplies that were there would be cut off. Bragg chose to protect his line of communication. He retreated to Cowan where he barely hesitated before retreating over the mountain.

As the troops retreated through Cowan, a woman came out on her porch and began berating the soldiers for withdrawing without a fight. Spotting Nathan Bedford Forrest, and not recognizing who he was, she shouted at him. "You big cowardly cur," she yelled. "If Old Forrest was here he would make you fight." Forrest rode on without comment, choosing to accept the insults than confront the angry woman.[120]

On the 2nd, Colonel Henry A. Hambright of the 79th Pennsylvania reported that the enemy had left the vicinity of the Elk River and was informed by rebel prisoners that their retreat was by way of Pelham and Cowan and across the mountains. That same day, General Phillip Sheridan started in pursuit of the Rebels on the road from Tullahoma to Winchester. When he reached the Elk River some three and a half miles from Winchester, he found the rain-swollen river impossible to ford. He turned his troops toward Allisonia (Estill Springs) until he reached Rock Creek, which also was also overflowing its banks. Eventually, he found a ford across Rock Creek where he could cross Elk River. The ford was guarded by a regiment of Confederate Cavalry, but after a sharp skirmish, Sheridan's forces were able drive off the Confederate forces and cross the river.

---

[120] John Watson Morton, *Forrest's Artillery*, (Create Space: 2012), 110. Morton says: "The incident was never related in General Forrest's presence without embarrassing him." Also Found in *Bedford Forrest and his Critter Company*, Andrew Lytle.

The following day Sheridan's forces marched on Winchester, driving in Confederate pickets. He was met with a force of Wheeler's cavalry numbering about two hundred men. Sheridan ordered a charge, and the Rebel force retreated through town before making a stand at Boiling Fork Creek about a mile outside of Winchester. After a short, but fierce fight, the Confederate cavalry was driven back toward Cowan by the superior forces.

On the 3rd, General Thomas J. Wood learned that the bridge at Pelham, which Wilder had used earlier, was still intact. Wood later became infamous as the Union general who, obeyed the mistaken orders sent by General Rosecrans and took his division out of line at the Battle of Chickamauga, and thereby ensured a Confederate victory.

Wood's brigade hurried to Pelham for the bridge in Pelham. He was met by Confederate cavalry and fell back to burn the bridge. The Yankee infantry then stormed the bridge, driving the Rebels off before the fire was able to destroy the bridge.

Wood lost only one man from the 97th Ohio and was able to repair the bridge. He posted men to guard it and now the Union had an avenue to cross the Elk River and flank Bragg.

On July 3rd, a reporter with a Northern newspaper reported that General Crittenden's forces under the command of General J.B. Turchin had a "fierce fight with rebel cavalry in Pelham. The Rebel forces retreated and were pursued to Mr. Pennington's near Hawkerville (Alto, TN) where the Rebels "stood their ground … until Turchin and his men charged with sabers and the rebels gave way and fled."[121] Turchin, a native of the Ukraine, had been court martialed for his role in allowing his men to sack, pillage, and rape the citizens of Athens, Alabama in 1862. He was not convicted and was later promoted. His presence in the area was likely a foreboding sign for the people of Grundy, Franklin, and Coffee Counties.

The movement by Union troops was an attempt to attack Bragg's rear and prevent his retreat. The action of the Confederate cavalry prevented the attack and allowed Bragg time to retreat. Lt. Col. Webb of the 51st Alabama Mounted Infantry

---

[121] http://palni.contentdm.oclc.org/cdm/compoundobject/collection/saddle/id/417. July 3, 1863.

was mortally wounded along with approximately 20 other Union soldiers. Confederate losses were reported at fifty killed.

In Pelham, Wood learned from deserters and some citizens that the Rebel forces had left earlier in the morning. They were also able to learn that Forrest had spent the previous night in Pelham and had moved toward the foot of the mountain to cross over.

On the morning of July 4th, General Sheridan ordered a part of his command up the mountain to probe the Confederate defense. Chaplain Bunting, who was with the Texas Rangers defending the crest of the mountain, described what happened. "After sunup, the enemy . . . advanced in a sweeping charge . . . The enemy charged within 5 paces, when they received a volley which drove them back." The Confederates reformed their broken lines. When the Union soldiers advanced again, the Texas Rangers charged and a very severe "hand to hand fight" ensued and the Union troops were driven back again. "The enemy then advanced on our left flank by the railroad cut with a large body of dismounted men and on our right hand with a large body of cavalry. Seeing that they were vastly outnumbered and that they had delayed the advancing Union army long enough for the retreating Confederates to descend the mountain, the Confederate troops retreated to Sweden's Cove, where they camped for the night. Bunting estimated the Union losses at thirty men, including several officers. Bunting praised the bravery of the Texas Rangers but reported they lost some 25 horses and had several men killed, wounded, or captured.[122]

Colonel Louis D. Watkins, commanding the advancing Union forces, told a slightly different story. He described the initial action as a "brief skirmish of ten or fifteen minutes" after which his men were ordered to fall back and regroup. Then after a "brisk fight of a half to three-quarter of an hour, the enemy was forced back. They, however, retired slowly, and fought obstinately for every foot of ground." He reported only three soldiers killed along with several wounded, but that the number of Rebels killed was "far greater than ours."[123]

Polk's retreat turned south toward Burnt Stand (Jump Off Road) and descended into Sweeton's Cove by way of "The Levels." By the night of the 3rd, Polk Corps, accompanied by

---

[122] Chaplin R.F. Bunting, Houston Texas Tri-Weekly Telegraph, August 19, 1863.

[123] OR, Series 1, Vol. XXIII, Pt. 1 p..550.

General Buckner's army, traveled down the southwest side of Battle Creek. At the mouth of Battle Creek, Buckner turned south and crossed the river at Bridgeport. Polk's Corps crossed the Tennessee about a mile north of the mouth of Battle Creek, using a pontoon bridge and continued toward Chattanooga by way of the Shellmond and Whiteside's Depots. This is the general route of I-24 from Nickajack Lake to the I-24 rest area at the Georgia state line.[124]

While camped between Winchester and Pelham, Captain James E. Love of the *8th Kansas*, an adjunct under General Rosecrans, wrote about his experiences to his fiancée Molly.

We are scouting around for guerillas (sp) & something to eat – and stay fast in camp. A pretty camp we have on a smooth grassy lawn or pasture with little groves scattered over it, in one of which our shelters are pitched, in another the Quartermasters train & Hd. Qts., in another the Hospital & doctors with the men. Shelters in nice lines stretching out right and left – and every think kept as clean as a parlor – every leaf and chip picked up. We moved here on the 6th of July and soon got

---

[124] Ralph Thompson, *Civil War Troop Movement Across the Plateau Following the Tullahoma Campaign.*

http://grundycountyhistory.org/05_Res/CW/Movements_Across_the_Plateau_1863_Pts1-2.pdf.

comfortable... Genl Davis then ordered (as a favor) to go to the mountains next day and capture a large party of Guerillas (sp) there secreted. We went at two in the morning and got back before dark after the most disagreeable day we have yet had – the hardest work too. Came near ruining all our clothes and Horses. It was climbing rocks & descending cliffs all day – caves abounded – and in them we chased these desperadoes. We only caught three, six horses, 2 mules and some contrabands, found Bacon & provisions, clothes, fires burning &c &c – but the main body we missed in the caves – and as soon as we passed they started to the other side the mountains with all their splendid horses niggers &c and are now on the other side of the Tennessee River. We got back safe with our plunder & so tired we slept all next day and did not recover for two or three days.[125]

The next major obstacle for the Army of the Cumberland during their pursuit of the Army of Tennessee was the crossing of the Cumberland Plateau. Ascending the mountain was difficult for an individual, but for an army and all its wagons and artillery, it was almost impossible. The army began its move on August

---

[125] http://www.historyhappenshere.org/archives/7414 (Civil War Love Letters: July 18, 1863).

The term "Contraband" was often used to signify a slave though in this case it may not be true.

16, 1863, from multiple locations-- Winchester in the south all the way to McMinnville to the north, a distance of more than 50 miles.

The Union Army took six different routes to cross the Cumberland Plateau. This helped to reduce the logjams of troops on the rough and narrow roads and across the plateau. Wood's 1st Division movement originated at Hillsboro. Wood chose to march through Pelham and took Park(s) Road through present day Layne's Cove, then up the mountain to Tracy City. They moved throughout the day and night of August 17 and reached the top of the plateau, where they rested until mid-day on August 18, and then moved on to Tracy City.

Other members of the Army of the Cumberland climbed the Cumberland Plateau from Cowan. Henry Campbell of the 18th Indiana recorded his observations of the climb up the mountain. After a rough climb over steep, rugged roads littered with trees cut by the retreating Confederates, Campbell reached the flat top of the plateau. Looking at the valley below, he called it the "grandest sight I ever witnessed. We were above the clouds of rain while the sun was shining brightly-making hundreds of rainbows on the side of the mountain beneath us-occasionally the clouds would break away and let us catch a glimpse of a most beautiful landscape." He camped at University Place and marveled at the "pure spring water that ran on top of the mountain." Campbell marveled at the view of the "country N.E. of Decherd," but complained that the "rattlesnakes are thick." He continued and passed through Tracy City, which he described as "three houses and a depot for the coal mine."[126]

At the same time as the skirmish at University Place was occurring, Rousseau's division marched to the Decherd and Pelham road and took up a position at Featherstone's. Negley, also using the protected bridge at Pelham, took up a position at Brakefield Point.

Reynolds' division encamped at Pennington's, and Brannan's division at Taite's; the two latter positions on the Decherd, Winchester, and McMinnville road. The order to halt was received at 2 p.m. this day, and the details for the repairs of roads were ordered. Location of corps headquarters was on the

---

[126] *Diary of Henry Campbell, Three Years in the Saddle*, August 16th-19th, 1863. https://opinionator.blogs.nytimes.com/2013/08/16/across-the-cumberlands/\ http://www.civilwarhome.com/links6.html

[128] Ibid, July 4, 1863.

Winchester and McMinnville road, half way between Tate's and Pennington's.

A Northern reporter traveling with Rosecrans' army described Tullahoma. I had "fancied it to myself as a romantic little town amongst the mountains, and lo it is a miserable village on a plain about as flat as the desert of Sahara." He continued that it had "no natural defenses . . . and either Decherd or Cowan is stronger." Still he conceded that Fort Rains was a "pretty good artificial defense. Double lines of rifle pits encircle the town" and on the "Manchester side the scrub oak forest was cut down over a space of several hundred yards wide, forming an almost impenetrable abates." In contrast to General Bragg, the reporter recognized the significance of the loss. There were "splendid crops of wheat and corn that cover all the hills and valleys in Middle Tennessee." It was nearing harvest time and to "lose . . . this miserable town was to lose the great storehouse and granary of the South."[128]

After the retreat of Southern troops from Tullahoma to Chattanooga, Union troops occupied Grundy County. Bragg tried to play down the significance of the loss of middle Tennessee. "Finding my communication greatly endangered by movements of the enemy, (Wilders raid on Decherd, made possible by the Union capture of the bridge at Pelham, enabled Union troops to cross the rain swollen Elk River and threaten Bragg's right. This was a significant development and played a crucial role in Bragg's decision to evacuate Tennessee.) I last night took up a more defensible position . . . losing nothing of importance."[127]

Despite Bragg's protest, Middle Tennessee was a crucial loss for the Confederacy. As historian Thomas Connelly has pointed out that the region of middle Tennessee was the heartland of the South. It made up much of what came to be known as the Heartland of the Confederacy. This area was a vital manufacturing area and "an irreplaceable source of raw materials, livestock, food, and other items."[128] The area also contained some of the most important railroad lines in the South, serving as arteries that connected most major cities west of the Appalachian Mountains. Through Tennessee flowed the Tennessee, Cumberland, and Mississippi Rivers that transported goods throughout the South. Without the railroads and the river

---

[127] Braxton Bragg in explaining why he abandoned Tennessee.

traffic, commerce in the South ground to a halt. It is in the Heartland that the Army of Tennessee "was organized, drilled, fed, armed, and equipped." It was also in this area where most of the major battles were fought.[129] Many would come to regard the loss of the Tennessee heartland as the greatest mistake of the war. General Joseph Johnston would later say of *Bragg*, "I know Mr. [Jefferson] Davis thinks he can do a great many things other men would hesitate to attempt. For instance, he tried to do what God failed to do. He tried to make a soldier of Braxton Bragg."[130]

Confederate Nurse Kate Cummings recorded in her diary that fall that "Tennessee is now wholly at the mercy of the enemy . . . our losses have proved, and opened our eyes to the disagreeable fact, that one of our men is not equal to five of the enemy, as we first thought. No one for a moment will say that our troops have not fought with a determination and bravery that have never been surpassed in any army, and that they have not always been opposed to at least double their number. 'Still honor to whom honor is due.' I have never spoken to any of our men on

---

[128] Connelly, Thomas L. *Army of the Heartland: The Army of Tennessee, 1861-1862*. Louisiana State University Press, Baton Rouge. 1967, 3.
[129] Ibid. P. 4.
[130] https://civilwartalk.com/threads/quote-re-hood-a-coincidence.4632/

the subject who have not told me that the enemy have exhibited a bravery and determination worthy of a better cause."[131]

Rosecrans' brilliant outmaneuvering of Bragg received little national notice. "Even in Washington, the Tullahoma campaign made no impression. On July 5 [1863, Secretary of War Edwin] Stanton telegraphed Rosecrans the news of Union victories at Gettysburg and Vicksburg . . . You and your noble army now have the chance to give the finishing blows to the rebellion. Will you neglect the chance?"[132]

Rosecrans was obviously displeased with the letter and fired back at Stanton. "You do not appear to observe the fact that this noble army has driven the Rebels from Middle Tennessee, which my dispatch informed you. I beg . . . do not overlook so great an event because it is not written in letters of blood."[133] Rosecrans was right, at least to some degree. The Union army had won a great victory that was as important as Vicksburg or

---

[131] Kate Cumming, *Kate: The Journal of a Confederate Nurse*. Richard B. Harwell, Editor. (Baton Rouge, 1959; orig. ed. ,1866). 111.

[132] Quoted in unpublished Master's Thesis: *The Tullahoma Campaign, The Beginning of the End for the Confederacy*, Major Julian D. Alford, Marine Corp University, 34.

[133] William Rosecrans to Secretary of War Edwin Stanton, 1863.

Gettysburg in determining the outcome of the war. The fact that it was accomplished with a minimal loss of life diminished its importance in the eyes of the public, but the astute observer realized the impact it had on ending the war. The Army of the Cumberland suffered only 550 casualties during the campaign and would likely have cut off Bragg's escape route across the Cumberland Mountains had it not been for the incessant rain and resulting mud that slowed his army's march.

However, others noted that Rosecrans had failed to achieve his objective, the destruction of the Confederate Army. Henry Cist, one of Rosecrans' staff officers, summed up the Tullahoma Campaign. "Brilliant campaigns without battles do not accomplish the destruction of an army . . . . A campaign like that of Tullahoma always means a battle at some other point."[134] That next battle would be at a small creek in Georgia known as Chickamauga Creek, and it would be one of the bloodiest days of the war and would result in the removal of General Rosecrans.

---

[134] Steven E. Woodworth, *Six Armies in Tennessee* (Lincoln: University of Nebraska Press, 1998), 43.

Thus, with remarkably few casualties, Bragg had allowed Federal occupation of all Middle Tennessee. The heartland of the confederacy was now firmly in Union hands and would remain under their control for the rest of the war.

The loss of Middle Tennessee was a demoralizing blow. Desertion, especially by native Tennessee troops, soared. Many questioned Bragg's leadership. One biographer has summed up Bragg's shortcomings:

Handicapped by poor health, he had no real taste for combat . . . Nor did he have the ability to inspire confidence in his subordinates. Notoriously inept at getting along with people he disliked, he simply could not win the loyalty of his chief lieutenants. ... contemptuous of volunteers and a democratic military establishment, he was unsuited to lead an army of individualistic citizen-soldiers. A mediocre tactician, he seemed unaware of the technical changes that had outdated pre-war assault tactics and strengthened the advantage of defensive combat.[135]

---

[135] Grady McWhiney, *Braxton Bragg and Confederate Defeat*, 1, 390.

Foraging

General Crittenden explained the occupation of Grundy County. *Manchester, Tenn., July13, 1863.*

SIR: On the morning of the 1st of July, I was ordered to form on the left of General Thomas, about 6 miles from Manchester, holding one division in reserve.... Subsequently, on the same day, I received orders to march my command to Pelham, via Hillsborough. Orders were immediately sent to Generals Palmer and Wood to this effect. General Wood reached Hillsborough that night, and Pelham next day at 12 m. General Palmer could not move that night, because in moving out to form in line of battle he had to cross an almost impassable swamp, and artillery and ammunition wagons had to be dug out of the mud. That night the direction of General Palmer's march was changed by an order from department headquarters, and next day he moved to Hart's tanyard.

I accompanied General Wood's division to Pelham. Near to Pelham we encountered a small force of rebel cavalry. They offered but slight resistance and were driven back so rapidly that the bridge which they had fired was seized, the fire extinguished, and the bridge saved. One hour after my arrival at Pelham 1 received an order from the general commanding the department to send General Wood to Hillsborough. The men being weary and the atmosphere oppressive, I did not order the return of General Wood and his command till 6 p.m.

On the morning of the 3d, at 6.30, just as General Wood reported in person with his command from Pelham, I received your order of 1.30 a.m. of the same day, directing me to proceed to Pelham with Wood's division, to intercept any portion of Bragg's force endeavoring to escape that way, and advising me of the position of General Palmer's command. After consultation with General Wood, I concluded to delay his return to Pelham until 10 a.m., when, no further orders arriving, he marched back to Pelham, I am remaining at Hillsborough with my staff, being at a point nearly equidistant from the two divisions in the places assigned to them.

General Palmer, at the suggestion of General Stanley, moved from Hart's tan-yard to support him with his cavalry in crossing Elk River, but the enemy having left, General Palmer returned to his camp. At 5.15 p.m. of the 7th, I received your dispatch of the 4th, dated Estill Springs, directing me to occupy McMinnville, Manchester, and Hillsborough, and, if practicable, Pelham with one brigade. I at once issued orders to General Beatty, then at Manchester, to rejoin his division, then at McMinnville; to General Palmer to march in the morning to Manchester, to relieve General Beatty, and to General Wood to occupy Hillsborough, leaving one brigade at Pelham. These orders were promptly complied with and show the relative position of my command at this date.

For more detailed information of the movements of my command since leaving Murfreesborough, I refer to the accompanying reports of Generals Palmer and Wood.

General Van Cleve, who left Murfreesborough on the 7th, with orders to occupy McMinnville, reports in two lines having taken peaceable possession of the place on the 9th.

Throughout the march officers and men of my command were cheerful and soldierly, though our part in this movement was as inglorious as it was disagreeable. I hope, however, that the presence of my command contributed somewhat to the general success.

I am, sir, very respectfully, your obedient servant,

T. L. CRITTENDEN, Major-general, Commanding.

Brig. Gen. JAMES A. GARFIELD, Chief of Staff, Department of the Cumberland.

The commander of the 21st Wisconsin Volunteers, camped between Pelham and Decherd, described a typical forage: We "went out 12 miles into the country, picked up all the corn I could find, then went to killing cattle, sheep, hogs, and chickens, wherever I could find them. Had lots of fun, went into every house I saw, and they would all lead strong, but I told the men to load the wagons . . . go to the smokehouses and take hams and shoulders or side meat or anything that could be found to eat.[136]

Typical of the plunder that faced the citizens of Grundy County was a letter written by a woman from nearby Winchester, Tennessee. "Houses in town ...were robbed. They gave leave to their troops to wander up and down the country, like devils, seeking what they might devour. The consequence was, that they carried on a system of general plunder, taking meat, meal, and flour, and other provisions . . . leaving nothing to eat, making a large majority of people wholly dependent on the enemy for rations"[137]

Private Alva Griest who was guarding a forage train just southwest of Pelham described his success. I "got six chickens, ½ bushel apples, ½ bushel of potatoes and three canteens on milk." He bragged about acquiring a "revolver, a carbine, and a fine silver mounted rifle and about three bushels of Confederate money unsigned."[138]

---

[136] Hiram Russell, 21st Wisconsin, to his wife and family, July 10th, 1863.
[137] Dr. Michael Bradley, Interview 2005.
[138] *Blue Lightening*, 60-61.

Wilder's men roamed as far on the Cumberland Plateau as Beersheba Springs. Private Joshua Foster of Company I of the 72nd Indiana Cavalry described Beersheba as "a place of restoration and summer resort for the big bugs of the South." The Griest found Beersheba to be a "beautiful place." Griest also found a horse hid in a cave. Their expedition in and around Grundy County enabled them to acquire about 1,500 animals during the six days.[139]

Beersheba diarist Lucy Virginia French described Wilder's venture to Beersheba. "In dashed a company of Yankees, Wilder's Cavalry and we were environed by the "blues" once more." Her husband went out and brought Wilder in to prevent more damage. All the Yankees took were a few "peaches" and "Chickens, which are a ruling passion with the Yankees." Searching for valuables that locals tended to hide below the bluff, they "broke into everything-outhouses, kitchens, bowling salons, etc. . . . amused themselves by pulling down chandeliers in the dining room and throwing ink bottles against the wall in the office- setting up bottles of wine upon the long piazza and rolling nine-pin balls at them . . . cutting the green cloth from the elegant

---

[139] *Blue Lightening*, 64.

billiard tables . . . and other capers of like caliber such as distinguished Yankees wherever they go." [140]

Though there were regulations about foraging, they were often ignored. As the war went on, the rules of engagement were stretched to allow more leeway. General Order No. 38 is an example of one of the many orders dealing with plundering of the citizens of occupied territories. "It has become necessary to call especial attention to existing orders for the suppression of straggling, pilfering, and improper and unauthorized intrusion on private property in the country occupied by our troops. The General disclaims any intention to spare or protect the property of disloyal citizens; on the contrary [he] is determined to the extent of his authority to appropriate it to the use and benefit of the troops in his command." It is vague at best and leaves open the question of how you determine which person is a loyal citizen. Reports of outrages against citizens were often overlooked, especially if the citizens were Confederate

---

[140] Lucy Virginia French, *The Beersheba Diaries of Lucy Virginia French*,.13.

sympathizers.[141] Most officers dismissed the plundering like Colonel Wilder who said there were "rogues" in every regiment.

As a soldier in Rosecrans' army wrote home that "when some of the boys get holt of any property belon[142]{g}ing to the rebels they destroy it as fast as they can and then say dam him he is the coss of bringing us here." Many other letters bragged of robbing from rich "sechs" and destroying their property. More than most areas of Grundy County, Pelham felt the hard hand of war. Union troops camped at Pelham over an extended period in 1862 and 1863. Supplying an army that size stripped the countryside of food and livestock. When Union troops moved on toward Chattanooga in 1863, soldiers burned the school, a church, and several houses. Earlier they had burned a tannery and saddle shop operated by Dan Patterson, located near Caldwell Bridge on the Elk River in Pelham.[143]

Margaret Davidson Gwyn, who lived at Blue Springs, which later became Viola, Tennessee kept a daily diary. She wrote, "I'm surrounded with danger but thank God he still

---

[141] General Order No. 38.

[142] Alva Grist Diary quoted in *The Hard Hand of War*, Mark Grimsley. 104.

[143] Arlene Partin Bean and Janelle Layne Coats, ED. *Homecoming 86: History of Elk River Valley*, (Manchester: Beaver Press, 1986.) 76, 93.

protects me." The Yankees [are] camped at McMinnville, Hillsboro and even Hubbard's Cove. On June 11, 1862, Margaret wrote, "Went to the store. Heard there were 2,000 Yankees camped last night in Hubbard's Cove and were coming on this way. I didn't stay very long, felt uneasy. Heard later in the evening they were doing a great many bad things above here. Taking people's horses and provisions."[144]

Other accounts relate similar incidents. On March 3, 1871, Congress passed a special act allowing citizens to file claims for property taken by the army during the Civil War. A few residents of Hubbard's Cove filed petitions with the Commission of Claims. James Winton, Jr., filed a petition in Tracy City, Tennessee, with the Commissioner of Claims in Washington, D. C. on February 15, 1873, in the amount of $540.00. The petition states that James Winton lived in Grundy County when this claim occurred and that, "He has a claim against the United States for property taken for the use of the army of the United States, during the late rebellion." The petition further states, "That on or about the 21st day of September in the year 1863, on or near the town of Altamont in the County of Grundy and State of

---

[144] Diary of Margaret Davidson Gwyn, October 11, 1862.

Tennessee, one Calvin C. Brixey, whose rank or position was that of Captain in the U. S. Army, took from your said petitioner for the use of said army, one bay mare, five years old, of the value of one hundred and forty dollars. Your petitioner further says that on or about the 4th of July in the year 1863 at or near the town of Pelham, in the said county of Grundy and state of Tennessee, that one Genl. Wilder, whose rank was that of Brigadier Genl., U. S. Army, took from your petitioner two mules, three years of age, of the value of one hundred and twenty- five dollars each. Your petitioner further says that on or about the 15th of February, in the year of 1865, at or near the town of Pelham in the county of Grundy and state of Tenn. one Rawlston, whose rank or position was that of a Lieutenant in the U. S. Army took from your petitioner, one grey horse five years old of the value of one hundred and fifty dollars.

William E. Griswold also made a claim on March 4, 1878, for property taken during the Civil War. His statement said," My name is William A. Griswold my age forty-seven years and my residence in Grundy County Tennessee near Altamont and my occupation is that of a farmer and a miller. I am the claimant in this cause. I was born and raised in the State of Tennessee U. S. of

America." He said that he was the owner of four beef cattle that were taken by soldiers under the command of General Wood, and these soldiers were stationed or encamped at Hillsboro, Tennessee. William said that the cattle were taken "off the commons near my house in the summer of 1863." He said, "The cattle were large and fat and would have weighed altogether net, at least 1800 pounds."

William reported that the army's butcher admitted to receiving the cattle and having butchered them, but he refused to pay for the cattle. William said that the beef would have been worth eight and ten cents net per pound.[145]

William Griswold also made claim for twenty-five bushel of corn that was taken from his house by a wagon master under General Negley's command in the summer of 1862. He valued the corn at seventy-five cents per bushel making the total value $18.75.

Another claim made by Griswold stated, "The bay horse and brown mule was taken from me in the road in the afternoon

---

[145] All claims listed were filed with the Southern Claims Commission **https://www.archives.gov/files/research/naturalization/418-disapproved-southern-claims.pdf**. Information provided by Bettye Sherwood.

one day in February or March as well as I now recollect in year 1863. Having the wagon gear on them to hitching them to a wagon, they were taken by the part of Col. W. B. Stokes Regiment under command of Captain Blackburn. Stokes was at that time in close pursuit of a rebel raiding party who was passing through Grundy County." Griswold said that he was forced to give up the horses and was ordered to strip the gearing off the horses. He said that he protested the horses being taken to no avail. Griswold was left afoot and the soldiers went on in pursuit of the rebels. Griswold stated that at the time of this event Lewis Hardison, William Woodlee and David Franklin were with him and saw the mule and horse taken. Griswold said that he had paid $100.00 for the horse shortly before he was taken, and the mule was well worth $75.00.

In the questionnaire that William Harrison Lusk filled out after the Civil War, he gave information about losses that he and his mother had suffered. He said that during the Civil War his mother, Sarah Lusk, had lost two very good mules worth about $300. He said that she also lost other things "to numerous to mention." Lusk said that he lost the biggest part of his meat, a fine mare, two cows, one calf, and $500.

Margaret Gwyn wrote in her diary about the burial of her granddaughter, Myrtle Wooton:

"She was buried this evening here at our family graveyard. We were surrounded with Federals at the time, not privileged to see her body laid in the earth. Thank God Heaven is our hope for future happiness."[146]

On November 29, 1883, William Wooten testified in a case between Gentile Braley and his sister, Atlanta England. The deposition tells of property destroyed during the Civil War in Hubbard's Cove. When asked, "Do you know whether or not Gentile Brawley after the war repaired and reset the fences on the land?" William, age sixty-five years, answered, "Yes sir, he did." William was then told to, "State as near as you can what the value of said work was worth." William answered, "I should put it at $25.00. It is only guess work with me."

Another documented disruption in the lives of our early ancestors during the Civil War comes from Wesley Chapel Church records. An old Wesley Chapel Church register states

---

[146] Diary of Margaret Davidson Gwyn

that, "1864 no cession of Tennessee Conference held on account of Civil War."[147]

Michael Gallagher, an Irish immigrant, became a U. S. citizen in 1855 and purchased 100 acres near the Elk River in Pelham. One of the men who worked for Gallagher was Moses Phipps, who became an infamous part of the Brixey gang. Though he was a loyal Union man, Federal troops occupying Middle Tennessee took much of his livestock.

Gallagher filed claim for compensation for one yellow mule, 3 steers, 2 milk cows, 1 calf, 2 oxen, 1 good bay saddle horse, 6 acres of Irish potatoes, 30 acres of field corn, and 80 head of hogs for a total of $2737.00. Because he was a Union man, he was eventually reimbursed $476.00.

T.T. Levan of Tracy City filed claims for 100-bushel corn, 10 beef cattle, 3 tons of hay, 1 fine horse, 64 pork hogs all taken by McCook's division, Army of the Cumberland. Later he would file a similar claim that Col. W.B. Stokes' men and Capt. Raulston of the 5th Tennessee Cavalry foraged from his farm. The total of $3,649.00 was denied by the commission.

---

[147] Wesley Chapel Church Records, Information provided by Bettye Sherwood.

Solomon Goodman of Pelham also filed a claim with the Southern Claims Commission for damages to his crops and property and theft of his livestock totaling the amount of $4,308.00. The commission denied his claim because they felt he was not a loyal Union man from the beginning of the Civil War and only swore the "Oath of Allegiance" after Union troops occupied Pelham. Such tales were played out throughout the county.[148]

In September of 1863, 4000 Federal troops of Brigadier James G. Spears' division, under the command of General William B. Stokes, were camped at Beersheba. Various units remained at Pelham, and the 20th Connecticut was stationed at Tracy City.

Future president James A. Garfield issued an order to Stokes from General Rosecrans:

September 24, 1863
Col. W.B. Stokes,
Commanding Cavalry, Tracy City:

---

[148] Jim D. Gallagher, *The Heritage of Grundy County TN 1844-2004*, (Memphis: Walsworth Publishing Co., 2004), 196-197. Sharon Goodman, Ibid. 206.

The general commanding directs that you proceed at once with the forces with which you have been operating in the Sequatchie Valley and report to the commanding officer at Bridgeport for scouting duty along the river below that place.

Leave one company at Tracy City, unless you can find Captain Brixey, who commands a company of independent scouts. If you find him, order him to protect that place, and then take your whole force with you.

J.A. Garfield

Brigadier-General, Chief of Staff[49]

In the early spring of 1865, Major A.W. Billings, who also served as Provost-Marshal, wrote to Maj. Gen. Milroy, Commanding Provost Marshall of the 1st Sub-District of Middle Tennessee, reported the organization of Home Guard companies in most of the local middle Tennessee counties. These Home Guards had greatly decreased the amount of "marauding, guerrillas, and the many small parties of robbers who formerly infested these counties." He singles out Coffee County and parts of Franklin County as being almost totally free of these

---

O.R., Series I, Volume XXX, Part 3, p. 835.

undesirables, but does not mention Grundy County, implying that such activity was still going on there.[150]

Despite the presence of the Union Army, bushwhackers, deserters, and other criminal elements roamed the countryside, outside the army's control, preying on individuals. At other times, these individuals operated with the army's permission.

Like Tennessee, Grundy County experienced divided loyalties. Some were conditional Unionists who switched allegiances according to who was in control of the area. Some were passive in their resistance while other Loyalists refused to shift their loyalty from the United States. Some hard-core Unionists defied Confederate rule, bushwhacked troops, stole from their neighbor, hid Union soldiers, spied for the Union, and did what they could to help the Union cause.

Captain Brixey is the infamous bushwhacker Calvin Brixey, a member of the Alabama-Tennessee Vidette Cavalry, a loose confederation of guerrillas and deserters who robbed and plundered much of the area.

[150] OR, Series I, Vol. 31, pt. III, pp. 292-293.

Deserters, home guards, and draft dodgers made up the irregular forces that preyed on civilians. Often no more than a band of robbers, these groups exacted revenge on neighbors for some real, imagined or unintentional slight or action. The results were often deadly.

The freedom of the irregulars depended chiefly in their association with the military command. Morgan's Raiders and Mosby's Rangers followed orders from the Confederate High Command but were allowed some latitude. Units outside the realm of command, like Quantrill's guerrillas in Missouri, acted completely on their own, following orders from their leaders and no one else.

Operating essentially on their own, these men caused difficulties for the Confederacy. The problems ranged from desertion and disobedience of orders to criminal acts aggravating the image of the South in northern minds. At first these problems led to anti-Partisan sentiments in the military hierarchy and eventually to sanctions and measures enacted to limit their activities. But the most pressing problem was desertion.

The summer of 1863 has often been described as the tuning point of the Civil War. In the East, Robert E. Lee, flush with confidence after Confederate victory at Chancellorsville, Virginia in May 1863, led the Army of Northern Virginia into Pennsylvania in hopes of winning a decisive victory and getting foreign powers to pressure the United States government to recognize the independence of the Confederacy. The result was the largest battle ever fought in North America, involving around 85,000 men in the Union's Army of the Potomac under Major General George Gordon Meade, and approximately 75,000 in the Confederacy's Army of Northern Virginia, commanded by General Robert Edward Lee. Casualties at Gettysburg totaled 23,049 for the Union (3,155 dead, 14,529 wounded, 5,365 missing). Confederate casualties were 28,063 (3,903 dead, 18,735 injured, and 5,425 missing), more than a third of Lee's army.[151]

The most memorable assault of the Battle of Gettysburg is commonly known as Pickett's Charge. On the third and final day of the Battle of Gettysburg, in a small town in central Pennsylvania, Lee made a tragic decision. Discouraged by two days of indecisive fighting, General Robert E. Lee decided to launch an attack on the center of the Union line, with the aim of splitting the Union line in half.

---

[151] http://www.historynet.com/battle-of-gettysburg.

Confederate General James Longstreet, second in command to Robert E. Lee during the battle, was Pickett's commander. He disagreed with Lee's decision to attack the strongly fortified position, but nevertheless obeyed orders and ordered Pickett to attack.

The assault line of the approximately 12,500 Confederate soldiers engaged in the attack extended a half-mile in width. The Rebels had to advance one mile through an open field and over a stone fence before they could engage their enemy. The greater part of this distance was through an open field where Union troops poured deadly cannon and rifle fire upon them. The Union troops maintained a murderous hail of rifle fire by organizing themselves into efficient lines four soldiers deep. After the first soldier in line fired, he would move to the back of the line to reload his weapon while the next soldier in line fired. Pickett's Charge briefly penetrated the Union line but was driven back with severe losses.

Of the estimated 12,500 Southern men to make this charge, about 54 percent (6,750) Southerners were killed, wounded, or captured in this one attack alone. Andrew Jackson Phipps of

Pelham was one of the survivors of Pickett's fateful charge.[152] As a disheartened Confederate, Major General George Pickett retreated toward the rear. General Lee met him asking him to reform his Division. General Pickett, devastated by what he had just witnessed, morosely responded to his commander, "General Lee, I have no Division now."[153]

Lee retreated to Virginia. It is estimated 51,000 soldiers were killed, wounded, captured, or listed as missing after Gettysburg. More than half that number was Confederate troops. While the North with its greater population could replace their casualties, the South was devastated by the losses. The Battle of Gettysburg is one of the most debated events of the Civil War. Sometimes referred to as the "Everlasting if" — what might have been if the outcome had been different — Gettysburg spelled eventual doom for the Army of Northern Virginia, as well as the hopes of an independent Southern nation.

At the same time Lee was retreating into Virginia, U.S. Grant was taking Vicksburg. After a prolonged siege, the

---

[152] Edwin Burnett, "The Early Days-Grundy County," *(The Heritage of Grundy County Tennessee)* 3-4.
[153] http://scienceviews.com/parks/pickett.html.

Mississippi River was under Union control, and the Confederacy was split in half.

In November of 1863, President Abraham Lincoln was invited to deliver remarks, which later became known as the Gettysburg Address, at the official dedication ceremony for the National Cemetery of Gettysburg in Pennsylvania. Lincoln delivered what many consider to be his most eloquent speech:

Four score and seven years ago our fathers brought forth on this continent, a new nation, conceived in Liberty, and dedicated to the proposition that all men are created equal.

Now we are engaged in a great civil war, testing whether that nation, or any nation so conceived and so dedicated, can long endure. We are met on a great battle-field of that war. We have come to dedicate a portion of that field, as a final resting place for those who here gave their lives that that nation might live. It is altogether fitting and proper that we should do this.

But, in a larger sense, we can not dedicate – we can not consecrate – we can not hallow – this ground. The brave men, living and dead, who struggled here, have consecrated it, far above our poor power to add or detract. The world will little note, nor long remember what we say here, but it can never forget what they did here. It is for us the living, rather, to be dedicated here to the unfinished work which they who fought here have thus far so nobly advanced. It is rather for us to be here dedicated to the great task remaining before us – that from these honored dead we take increased devotion to that cause for which they gave the last full measure of devotion – that we here highly resolve that these dead shall not have died in vain – that this nation, under God, shall have a new birth of freedom – and that government of the people, by the people, for the people, shall not perish from the earth.[154]   *Abraham Lincoln November 19, 1863*

---

[154] http://www.abrahamlincolnonline.org/lincoln/speeches/gettysburg.htm.

Brixey and Other Bushwhackers

A Great Revival swept through Confederate camps during the winter of 1863-1864. There was a massive outpouring of evangelical religion not seen since the Great Revival of 1801. Perhaps the suffering and failure of the Confederate Army in the west led to the rise of religious fervor. "Our sins must have been great," wrote Confederate nurse Kate Cummins, "to have deserved such punishment."[155]

War forced soldiers to face their mortality. Every day they faced the possibility of stepping out into eternity. The fear of death and their awareness of the fragility of life forced many young men to prepare their soul for eternity. This belief of a future afterlife enabled them to face the uncertainty of battle and the devastation of war. These revival tendencies were especially evident after battles, especially Confederate losses.

The belief that their cause was just, and that God was on their side was nearly universal in the South. Losses in battle were explained as God's chastening, but ultimately most southerners

---

[155] *Kate Cummins Journal.*
https://loashared.s3.amazonaws.com/static/pdf/Cumming_Nameless_Dead.pdf.

believed that God would deliver them from the Philistines of the North.

In April 1864, President Jefferson Davis called for a day of prayer. Yankee success, many believed, was due to the spiritual failures of Southerners. A great revival broke out among Southern troops. There were thousands of converts. Bishop Leonidas Polk baptized many of the Confederate officers, including Generals Johnston, Hood, Hardee, and Bragg.

Not everyone was taken by the religious spirit. Bushwhackers with allegiances to either side roamed the area in and around Grundy County. Often, they switched sides depending on which army was in control of the area. "The truth is each side, when it gets a little the advantage and gets those on the opposite party trodden down a little, crows a little too big, and when the trodden down party gets a chance to, {it}retaliates rather severely."[156]

On September 4, 1863, two men fired on two Union soldiers just north of Hillsboro, TN. One soldier was killed and both soldiers were robbed. Just why the soldiers were alone and away from the rest of their platoon was never established. Likely, they

---

[156] Amanda McDowell. *Fiddles in the Cumberland's*. 203.

were stragglers who were searching for something to steal. John W. Johnson and Alexander P. Anderson were arrested and tried for the crime. Johnson was sentenced to be hanged. Anderson was found guilty, but with mitigating circumstances, and sentenced to five years in the state penitentiary."[157]

For the most part, the bushwhackers were nothing more than bands of deserters, robbers, and killers who saw the war as an opportunity for personal gain and vengeance. "Those who tried to protect their property or show resistance were abused, threatened, their property burned, and even whole families slain in cold blood."[158]

One of the main threats to citizens of Grundy came from Cal Brixey. Cal was the son of Johanna McGehee and John Oliver Brixey. He was born in 1839 near Viola, Tennessee. John had been killed February 7, 1846, in Mexico while serving in the Mexican War. Cal married Martha E. Swann in Vervilla, Tennessee near Viola on March 4, 1858. By 1860 they had two small children.

---

[157] Michael Bradley, *With Blood and Fire: Life Behind Union Lines in Middle Tennessee*, 186165, pp. 38-39.

[158] Ibid. P.229.

Cal Brixey enlisted in the Confederate Army, Company C, of Col. John Savage's 16th infantry regiment in Lynchburg, TN on July 29th, 1861. After the battle of Shiloh, he was listed as a "deserter now bushwhacking in Middle Tennessee."

After 1862, Brixey had a change of allegiance. In 1863 he formed a company of Union supporters and was commissioned captain in Company D of the Alabama-Tennessee Vidette Cavalry, which was headquartered in Hubbard's Cove, their camp being less than 100 yards from the Cumberland Mountains. Their assignment was to patrol the area from Altamont to Jasper. They were described as a "company without discipline and a lawless set of men."[159]

Brixey and his men terrorized, robbed, and murdered men in Grundy and nearby counties. Jim Burnett, born in Pelham in 1910, recalled family stories about his grandfather Johnny Burnett and other local citizens of Grundy County being threatened by the Brixeyites. Johnny was ordered to get a wagonload of corn and take it to Brixey and his men camped at the "Patton Place,"

---

[159] LeRoy P. Graf and Ralph W. Haskins, Ed., *The Papers of Andrew Johnson: 1862-1864* Volume 6, (Knoxville: The University of Tennessee Press, 1983.) 391.

the home of Alexander Patton. It was to be used to feed their horses. One of the men was in the barn watching his as he loaded the corn. Looking for something to steal, he walked into the stable where Johnny had a fine mare about to foal. The mare was lying down and Brixey's man, thinking the horse was old and lazy, kicked her and said, "Get up, Old Heavy!" The mare remained on the ground and the man left, satisfied that the mare was too old to bother with stealing. The man did not take the mare and she had a fine colt afterward.[160]

Some excerpts from Margaret Davidson Gwyn's Diary shed some additional light on events that were transpiring in Grundy County and surrounding areas.

Saturday July 11th 1863

Went to see dear-little Myrtle twice yesterday. Heard last night before we slept she was dead. Went over and saw her cold and lifeless body so different from yesterday. Free from pain now and at rest. Though it is so hard to give up our dear friends. She was buried this evening here at our family graveyard. We were surrounded with Federals at the time.

---

[160] Janice Burnett White, "*Brixeyites*," *The Heritage of Grundy County Tennessee* 1844-2004, 9.

Not priviledged (Sic) to see her body laid in the earth. Thank God in heaven is our hope for future happiness.

Sunday July 12th: Rose this morning and feeling very gloomy. Was foraged on all day. It looked like we were going to be deprived of any subtenance. (Sic) We have something yet. Thank God for his mercies.

Sunday, August 16th: This evening the Federals are camped all around us. The troops from Manchester are on their march to Chattanooga. We can't tell our feelings in our present condition. The Lord will provide. Thank him for his continued goodness.

October 14, 1863: Wednesday Mr. William Powell's house was burned by the USA bushwhackers. (William Powell was already dead. His wife, Mary Ann, and children, Elisha and Thomas, lived alone. Mary Ann Powell sent her little six-year-old son, Thomas, to hide behind a hill while she fought them alone. They took her feather bed and best mare and rode it away after burning the house.) Lord have mercy on us. I thank thee for our mercies.

October (a week later) Young Mr. Powell (Elisha) was killed today by the same crowd (bushwhackers) that burned his house last week. Mr. Ogle was killed at the same time. Remember us O Lord.[161]

---

[161] Diary of Margaret Davidson Gwyn

Quinn Powell of Manchester told about the death of his older brother Elisha:

Elisha Powell, only about 16 years old, had started from his house to buy a cow from a farmer. He had gone as far as the Frank Ragsdale place when he was overtaken by a group of bushwhackers from the mountain. They caught him and robbed him of $21. They ran him to the Joe Wileford place, and then told him to 'run for his life'. He started running and they began shooting. They shot him and then ran their horses over him.

The bushwhackers then went and told Jim Bryan they had 'shot a damn bushwhacker, and he had some good boots if he wanted then.

They had already burned the house where Elisha and his family lived. His father (William Powell, son of Alexander) was dead. His mother, Mary Ann (Douglass) Powell, sent her little six-year-old son, Thomas Guinn Powell, to hide behind a hill while she fought them alone. They took her feather bed and best mare and rode it away after burning the house. The bushwhackers, as best he remembered, were: Cal Brixey, George Hawk, ____ Hord (or Hard), _____Hampton, _____ Campbell, and _____Laws.[162]

---

[162] Coffee County Historical Quarterly Vol. XX June 1990, p. 22.

Another story recalled the time when Brixey and his men went to a home and demanded the woman living there fix a meal for them. While she was cooking, the men ransacked the house, stealing everything of value, even taking the feather mattress off the bed. The men started loading the wagon and the woman went into the bedroom to check on her baby that had been asleep. Not finding the baby, she screamed and ran outside to the wagon where she found the baby wrapped in the covers on the mattress they had stolen. The baby was returned unharmed, but all their household goods were taken.[165]

A letter from several citizens in the Pelham area noted the issues that they were having with Brixey and his men.

Near Pelham, Tn., Sep 1st A.D. 1863 Genrl G. D. Wagner, (George Day)

Dear Sir, We the undersigned citizens of Grundy County and Vicinity of Pelham be leave to state our grievances as a people to you and hopefully as that you take steps as you may think the nature of the case and circumstances demands since your departure from the neighborhood the company recently organized under Capt. Bricksy (Sic)have assumed authority to arrest quite citizens without any charge what ever have

---

[165] White, Brixeyites, p.9.

taken private property such as young horses and mules (not in any way wanted for the service) and appropriated them to their own private use all of this to us seems unwarranted and wrong and hoping that we have some claims to protection from the Federal Government . . .

Very respectfully Your obt Servants
S. P. Goodman
Thomas Harrison
Isaac Rust
A. S. Goodman
J. C. Walker
S. T. Witt [163]

---

[163] https://civilwartalk.com/threads/confederate-guerrilla-ancestors.84369/page-2

Brig. Gen. George Day Wagner was a politician without any military experience but became a capable general. He was born in Ross County, Ohio but his family moved to Warren County, Indiana when Wagner was still a child. He worked as a farmer while he pursued a political career. He was elected member of the House of Representatives on the Republican ticket in 1856. In 1860, he was elected to the state Senate, and served as president of the Indiana State Agricultural Society until the Civil War began. He volunteered his service in June 1861 and was commissioned a colonel and given a brigade in the Army of the Ohio. His first major battle was at Shiloh in the division of Gen. Thomas J. Wood. When the army was reorganized to the Army of the Cumberland, Wagner's brigade was named 2nd in Wood's first division.

Wagner's 2nd division had been camped at Pelham near the foot of the mountain for more than a month. He had been ordered to repair the road up the mountain known as Parks Road. General Wood had determined to cross the mountain through Pelham to Tracy City with his three divisions.

Apparently, the citizens of Pelham felt Wagner was the commander in charge of the troops in the area or serving as Provost Marshal.

Anderson S. Goodman, one of the signers of the petition, was later killed by three of Brixey's men. According to reports, Goodman surprised them as they were trying to steal his horses, but it may have been in part because of the letter he had written complaining about Brixey.

According to one report, the names of the murderers of old man Anderson Goodman were Mart. Phipps, – McChristian, and – Conatzy. The immediate cause was this: The old man was at a prayer-meeting one night, when these men shaved his mare's mane and tail. He met them on the Sunday following and upraided [sic; presumably upbraided] them for the act. They immediately reported him to the bloodthirsty Brixey, at Tracy City, and he sent a squad to kill him, which they did on the following Tuesday. He was taken from his plow and carried about a mile. Phipps and Conatzy did the shooting, one ball striking him in the brain and the other in the chest. They forbade his body to be touched or buried, but this attended to by the neighbors after the murderers left.[164]

Outraged local citizens petitioned General Lovell Rousseau in Nashville. Brixey was finally arrested by Federal authorities and sent to Nashville for trial. Although charged with several cases of murder and robbery, he was released from prison by the Federal Authorities on June 28, 1864, because no witnesses appeared to testify against him. It was reported that Brixey's men threatened anyone who dared to testify, and the provost marshal in Tullahoma, Robert Millroy, approved of Brixey's dealing with southern rebels and refused to grant travel passes to anyone who might have been brave enough to want to testify.[165]

Returning to his men, Brixey soon returned to his murderous ways. It was reported that he and his men killed another 18 men after his return. In September 1864, the Union Forces that had occupied Grundy County since 1862 had moved on, chasing what was left of the Army of Tennessee. Brixey and a few of his men, Jim Kenniatzen (Conatzy?), Martin Phipps and a man named Henry, rode to the school in (Hawkerville) Hockerville, present day Alto. Teacher J. P. Hindman reported

---

[164] http://www.1stusinfantry.org/articles/bloodyTN.html.

the incident that happened. "Brixey appeared a good deal under the influence of spirits." The reason for the visit was to kill a fifteen-year-old schoolboy named Jesse Abernathy who Brixey believed had stolen some brandy from him. Abernathy explained that he did not know that the brandy belonged to Brixey and that he would pay him for it. "Brixey then said that he himself individually had command of this country-that the Rebels might, it was true, come the next day and send him galloping to Hell, but he'd be G_ _ D_ _ _ _ d if he did not rule this country now." After terrorizing the school, Brixey accused Abernathy and his father of being "Secesh" and he didn't intend for any "Secesh" to live in this country. He arrested Abernathy and another boy and started to the woods toward Decherd, presumably to kill him.[166]

They were intercepted by a regiment of Joe Wheeler's Confederate cavalry, led by Captain Paul Anderson. Brixey and his men released Abernathy and made a run for safety. Kenniatzen (likely Conatzy) and Phipps's horses jumped a palling fence, but Brixey's horse was unable to jump the fence and he was captured, and Henry killed. Brixey claimed that his

---

[165] Civil War Soldiers in Coffee County, TN
[166] Union Provost Marshall's Records, MC 345, Roll 129. Found also in Bradley's *With Blood and Fire.* 111-113.

name was Stokes and he was from Lebanon but he was recognized by several members of Anderson's command.

Brixey was carried to his mother's house in Manchester to say his final goodbyes. His wife came and begged for mercy. Having heard the atrocities committed by Brixey, the Confederate cavalry was in no mood to be sympathetic. Brixey's boots were removed and he was tied bareback on a mule. His wife got a pair of socks and put on his feet. His mother wrung her hands, wept great tears and pleaded for his life. It was reported that his last recorded words were to tell his wife not to "cry, I'll be back." He was led a few miles out of town on the road toward Murfreesboro to a place called Big Springs. There a rope was placed around his neck, the ropes cut from his feet, and a switch to the back of the mule sent the most infamous bushwhacker in Grundy County into eternity.

Martin VanBuren Phipps (Phips) seems to have been Brixey's right-hand man. Phipps was born in 1843 in the Pelham Valley area. On December 1, 1862, he enlisted and was assigned to Co. G, 4th Confederate Regt., Tennessee Infantry. Army life apparently did not agree with Martin, and he is listed as "left sick at Manchester" on December 7, 1862. Two months later, he was listed as a deserter. He was back on the roll for March and April but deserted again.

On July 31, 1863, at Pelham, TN, C. Brixey recruited Martin to serve in the 1st Independent Co. D of TN, Volunteer Cavalry. Riding with Brixey as a member of the Vidette Cavalry placed Phipps in precarious positions. Brixey was the most hated and feared bushwhacker in the area, and Martin seems to have followed his lead without question. In September of 1864, Brixey was captured and eventually hanged. Martin escaped the noose and fled west, showing up on the 1870 census for Jack County, Texas, but later returned to Tennessee.[167]

An acquaintance of Brixey confirmed his demise several years after the war ended.

Altamont, March 30th, 1872

I, William H. Hampton, 1st Lieutenant of Company M, of the 10th Regiment of Tennessee Volunteers Cavalry, certify on honor that Captain Calvin L. Brixey was a Captain in the 1st Independent Cavalry,

---

[167] Information on Martin VanBuren Phipps from Jackie Layne Partin's, *Martin VanBuren Phipps, A Brixeyite,* found on the Grundy County, TN Historical Society website.

http://grundycountyhistory.org/03_Ind/Jackie/Phipps,%20Martin%20Van%20Buren%20Story.pdf.

and his widow is, as I am informed, an applicant for an army Pension; that by communication with most any Loyal Citizen near Dechard (sp) and the Department can get other information, corroborating with. And I further certify, that the said Calvin L. Brixey, was captured by the Rebel General Wheeler's command in Franklin County, Tennessee, 1864, while raising volunteers to go West. James Canaster and Martin Phips, two of Brixey's enlisted men was with him and escaped. Martian Phips now lives in Grundy County, Tennessee, and James Canaster lives some where in Kentucky. The Rebels taken Captain Brixey tied upon a horse near Murfreesborough and there they hung him by the neck until he was dead and then left him hanging by the neck forbidding the Citizens taking him down. He was hung on or about the 3rd of September, 1864 and remained there until about the 4th of September, 1864. I know that I'm not mistaken in the identity of Brixey. I was well acquainted with him.

William H. Hampton Late 1st Lieutenant Commanding Co M, 10 Tennessee Volunteer Cavalry[168]

Another of Brixey's men was also more fortunate. One local Pelham man, Spunky Bill Layne, who had ridden with Brixey, was captured and about to be hanged at the point on Cox

---

[168] http://www.1stusinfantry.org/articles/bloodyTN.html
http://home.freeuk.com/gazkhan/tenn_black-sheep.htm

Ridge near Billy Gilliam's house, but his kin who lived nearby begged for him to be spared. He wasn't hanged, but because of his association with Brixey, he was despised by the local community and even his own family.[169]

Just as the people in the valley were besieged by bushwhackers, people on the mountain faced similar issues, especially in Beersheba Springs. Lucy Virginia French reported in her diary that by August 1863 almost every man on the mountain had taken the 'oath of allegiance." Still, the "Home Guard as they style themselves-that is to say the Bushwhackers and Brigands in Yankee uniform ride in occasionally to see that we all are walking loyally and minding our oaths."[170] Their arrival usually meant they were expecting to be fed and their animals provided with hay and feed. French reported that two bushwhackers, Charlie Ainsworth, who Bloomfield Ridley described as a "Chicago Jailbird," and one Campbell seemed to be frequent visitors to Beersheba. They paraded around "dressed in the finest Yankee uniforms-stolen of course." Campbell had on the cap of Dick Smartt, a young man who had died earlier. Campbell had stolen

---

[169] Arlene Partin Bean and Janelle Layne Coats, ED. *Homecoming 86: History of Elk River Valley*, (Manchester: Beaver Press, 1986.) 96.

the cap out of Smartt's sister's trunk and went to her door so she could see him wearing her dead brother's cap.

Another one of these infamous guerrillas was Wilson "Wilts" Purdom. (Purdham) Wilson Purdom is listed on the 1860 census of Grundy County, Tennessee as being 42 years old. His wife Lydia is 35 and they have nine children. Their son Wiley is fourteen. No occupation is listed, though the land value is listed at $760.00.

According to Lucy Virginia French, Wilts Purdom had at one time been a member of General Ben Hill's regiment who deserted and "went to horse stealing, robbing, etc. on the mountain." Captain William Lewis and the 42nd Missouri routed Purdom's band at their camp near Altamont on February 5, 1865.[171] The next night, Lt. Haynes surprised Purdom and two others at Corn's farm, between Pelham and Hillsboro. Some accounts say he was arrested along with the two others and placed in irons. The two others escaped, but Purdom remained in captivity and was "lost" by orders of General Hill.

---

[170] Lucy Virginia French, *Diary of Virginia French*, 23.
[171] Ibid. Lucy Virginia French. *The Beersheba Diaries*. 12-13.

Many guerrillas were taken to the woods and executed and wound up being classified as lost. Purdom's men vowed revenge against Hill.

Benjamin Hill was born on June 13, 1825, the son of Isaac and Frances Pickett Hill, in the Irving College area of Warren County. His grandfather, Benjamin Hill, was a brother of Henry John Alexander Hill, the representative who presented the petition to create Warren County. His father died in 1834 when Ben was only nine years old. He borrowed the money to attend and graduate from Irving College, probably the most prestigious learning institute for miles around in that era. After graduating in 1844, he moved to McMinnville, entering the mercantile business. In 1857, he was elected state senator. When the war came, Hill was active in organizing units in the McMinnville area. He was elected Colonel in 1861 and took part in most of the major battles, from Shiloh to Franklin.

During Union occupation of Middle Tennessee, Hill's cavalry unit was under the command of Nathan Bedford Forrest. Hill had a house in Beersheba Springs and often made visits there to see his wife. Lucy Virginia French reported an interesting story that even though Wilts Purdom had made threats against

Ben Hill, Mrs. Hill was traveling with Wilts Purdom's son (Wiley) to meet her husband in the Sequatchie Valley. Wilts Purdom's men had threatened to kidnap Mrs. Hill and hold her for ransom. Two of Purdom's men, John Smartt and Charlie Ainsworth, an escaped convict from Illinois, were in Beersheba looking for young Purdom and Mrs. Hill soon after they left.

"Bushwhackers haunts were on the mountain and they visited Beersheba almost daily, stealing everything they could transport in wagons," reported Betty Ridley Blackmore, who was living in Beersheba during the summer of 1863.[172] "Any family there whose friends were South in the Army . . . and unoccupied cottages of southerners suffered severely." Mrs. Blackmore was the sister of Bloomfield Ridley, though her connection remained unknown to the various bushwhackers that invaded Beersheba from time to time. Her house was free from the plundering as she explained. "I appealed to the Captain of the Gang-Capt. Hard Hampton, for protection-told him we were two unprotected females, at Beersheba for our health-showed him our stack of

---

[172] Betty Ridley Blackmore, *Beersheba Springs: A History*. (The Beersheba Springs Historical Society, 1993),115.

provisions, etc.-and asked him to give orders to his men not to molest us, which he most magnanimously done."[173]

Mrs. Blackmore also reported that the Federal Army made four visits to Beersheba that summer looking for Rebels. She reported that as many as 200 Union soldiers descended on Beersheba, searching houses and grounds for Confederates. The incident she, as well as Virginia French, recall with the most horror is the "sacking of Beersheba by the natives of the mountain." Many of the bushwhackers lived in the relatively uninhabited areas on the mountain. On Sunday, July 26th, 1863, 7 or 8 armed bushwhackers accompanied by their family and friends rode slowly into Beersheba. They reported that the Federals were coming to burn the place and they might as well remove the things before the Yankees burned them. They brought their wagons, along with their wives and children, and began taking whatever they wanted from the cottages. They would demand the keys from Superintendent Tom Ryan and unless he produced it at once, they broke the doors down. Two women had a fight at one cottage over some articles. These natives were described as poor, ignorant and envious, dirty,

---

[173] Ibid.

squalid, and wicked talking wretches. Many stayed up all night tho' it was the Sabbath, they danced and drank all night.[177]

The sack of Beersheba lasted 3 days before the bushwhackers were ready to move on. The robbers claimed to be sanctioned by General George Day Wagner, Union Provost Marshal stationed in Hillsboro. The bushwhackers wore blue clothes and claimed to belong to the Union Army, but the Federals denied it and refused to do anything about the sacking.[174]

On September 4, 1863, the Memphis Bulletin reported that there was a "huge and enthusiastic meeting recently held in Grundy, in this state, at which resolutions were adopted disavowing the ordinance of secession and expressing a strong wish to return again to allegiance in the Federal government and become loyal citizens of the same."[175]

Where this meeting took place, if indeed it did occur, is never mentioned. Altamont or Tracy City seem to be likely places as Union sentiment ran strong in those areas.

---

[174] Ibid, also Information about the Sacking of Beersheba obtained from *Virginia French's Diary* July 26, 1863.
[175] Memphis Bulletin, Sept. 4, 1863.

Mrs. Ester Brasher, who grew up in Pelham and taught school for many years, related a story that had been handed down in her family since the war. "During the War Between the States, Yankee forces were camped all about Pelham. One bunch was camped at the old school which was just behind my house here. When they left a bunch set fire to the school and the church and burned it to the ground. They stole everything of any value, even quilts off people's beds and they burned the rest. It was a terrible hard time in Grundy County."[176]

---

[176] Mrs. Esther Brashear interview by author 1975.

Final Campaigns

The winter of 1863-1864 was extremely cold. Rivers and streams froze over, and a large amount of snow fell on the plateau. In January of 1864, Confederate Major Scott Bledsoe led his command in to Grundy County. Bledsoe was technically a part of General Joe Wheeler's command, but having been separated from Wheeler, he spent much of the latter part of the war with Colonel John Hughes [Hughs] and Captain George Carter, raiding behind Union lines. In August 1863, General Bragg had issued Order No. 217 authorizing Hughes to round up deserters and those dodging conscription. Homegrown "Torries" populated the plateau, especially after the success of the Union Army in Middle Tennessee.[177]

John Hughes was a hotel operator in Livingston, TN in Overton County before the war. He was described as a "stout, active, athletic man, and one of the best marksmen in the

---

[177] James B. Jones Jr., *Hidden History of the Civil War: Tennessee*, (Charlestown and London: History Press: 2013), 64.
OR Series 2, Vol. 15 166-67; 671-82.

Confederate Army." He rose to the rank of Colonel in the 25th Tennessee Infantry despite receiving low scores from his superiors for lax discipline and poor administration. He participated in several important battles, including the invasion of Kentucky, Stones River, and Hoover's Gap.

Carter's home base was in Spencer, Tennessee in nearby Van Buren County. Carter, a blacksmith by trade, commanded a battalion of mounted scouts loosely associated with Wheeler's cavalry. Carter was hot tempered and courageous. He had been captured in 1863 and sent to Fort Delaware Prison where he promptly escaped, swam across the bay, and returned to action in Chattanooga. Carter and his men spent a great deal of time in Grundy County when Union forces were searching for him in his home county. Hughes, Carter, and Bledsoe were familiar with Grundy County and had widespread support in the area.

Albert "Hootie" Knight recalled hearing stories from his grandfather Dolphin Knight about his encounter with a band of Rebels. Young Dolphin was walking out of Savage Gulf early one morning to go to work at a sawmill. Crossing a creek and coming to an open field, he came upon a band of Rebel soldiers. At the time, most of Middle Tennessee was occupied by Union troops, so he thought the encounter strange. They invited him to share in their breakfast. The smell of bacon and coffee was enough to convince him. As they ate breakfast, the men asked him if he had seen any Yankee patrols. After breakfast, the men rode toward Altamont. He estimated that there must have been about 200 men. More than likely, this was Bledsoe and his men.[178]

Bledsoe was described by a fellow soldier as "a true and brave soldier and a most affable and intelligent gentleman."[179] He arrived in Altamont early in the morning of January 20, 1864. He would later write that he had learned from informants that two 'homegrown" Yankees were in Altamont. The command rode up to the house of Captain Stephen Tipton of the 1st Alabama and Tennessee Vidette Cavalry, who was in Grundy County recruiting men for the Union Army. Stephen P. Tipton is listed on the 1860 Census of Grundy County, Tennessee as being 28 years old and living in District 10. He was the son of a prosperous Grundy County farmer Jonathan Tipton. The Tiptons

---

[178] Author interview with Albert "Hootie" Knight, 2014.

[179] George B. Guild, *4th Tennessee Cavalry Regiment*, (Cool Springs Press, Nashville, 1913), 184.

[180] http://grundycountyhistory.org/05_Res/Reports/Transcription%20of%20Nicholson's%20Articl es.pdf.

were connected with Adrian Northcutt's family, both by land investments and by marriage. Stephen married Louisa Elisabeth Griswold, the daughter of Stephen M. and Sarah Purdom Griswold. Sarah was the sister of noted guerrilla, robber, and bushwhacker Wilson "Wilts" Purdom.[180]

When Captain Tipton and Private David Franklin emerged from his house, they spotted the rebel troops and tried to get back inside but were gunned down. Tipton was described as a man who had got up a company of "Home Guard" and had been pressing and stealing provisions, forage, etc. from people in the valley.[181] His connections to Purdom and his likely mistreatment of Confederate sympathizers likely led to his death.

The main target of Bledsoe's attack was the Yankee garrison at Tracy City. The command there consisted of 2 commissioned officers and 72 enlisted men from the Twentieth Connecticut Volunteers. Also present were 1 officer and 73 enlisted men from Captain Tipton's command; few were armed with anything but a few squirrel rifles.

---

[181] Janelle Taylor, Ed., *The Heritage of Grundy County, TN*. (The Grundy County Historical Society: Walsworth Publishing, 2004), 397.

[181] Lucy Virginia French, 34.

The Confederates stormed into Tracy City before the pickets' alarm could be sounded. They rode in at the back of Howard and Benham's store, firing as they rode by, killing Private David B. Powell of the 20th Connecticut Volunteers. Soldiers inside the store returned fire. The Rebel force moved to the railroad depot. Captain Andrew Upson was there with a guard of three men. Upson attempted to join his command, but seeing the way blocked, he and his men attempted to flee into the woods. He was quickly surrounded; he threw down his pistol, but was wounded before the firing stopped.

Lieutenant Jepson, the second in command, rallied the remaining troops in the stockade near the store. The Rebel cavalry turned their attention once again to the storehouse. They formed a line of battle under cover of an elevation of ground to the right of the stockade, and under like cover in the rear of the railroad depot, and still another portion farther to the left and in the rear of the engine-house. In this covered position, they were completely sheltered and any fire from the stockade was ineffectual.[102]

---

[182] O.R. Series I, Volume XXXII/1

Major Bledsoe sent a message demanding surrender. Having a good defensive position, and not affected by enemy fire, Lieutenant Jepson declined. Unable to breech the stockade, the Rebel troops burned the engine house and building covering the coal chutes. They remained in that position until dark, and fearing Union reinforcements from Cowan, they then left Tracy City. They spent the night a few miles from Tracy near the house of David Nunley and then retreated through Altamont and Beersheba toward White County.

S. M. Smith of the 20th Connecticut was with Upson when he was wounded. Upson was carried to the depot and given medical care. For several days he appeared to be getting better, dictating a letter to his wife telling her he was confident of recovery, but developed an infection and died. In a letter to Upson's wife after the Captain's death, Smith described Upson as a "noble husband, sincere friend, and efficient officer."[183]

Smith described how Upson "took an interest in the welfare of the people about here." As Tracy City did not have a school,

---

[183] S.M. Smith to Mrs. Andrew Upson April 10th, 1864. http://www.southingtonlibrary.org/CivilWarLetters/Civil%20War%20Letters%20Transcriptions/

Upson set up a school in one of the depot rooms and appointed one of his soldiers as teacher. He even offered to procure books for those that did not have them.[184]

A devoutly religious man, Upson wrote of hoping to spend Thanksgiving with his wife and children. Like many from both North and South, he never got to realize his dreams.

Jepson notified his superiors of the attack, claiming that 100 to 150 men, "a portion of which force is known as Captain Joe Carter's cavalry" had attacked the garrison. Most likely, Joe Carter was Captain George Carter, a well-known irregular cavalry officer whose home base was between McMinnville and Beersheba Springs. Carter, Hughes, and Bledsoe's men often rode with each other when a larger body of soldiers was needed.

Learning of the attack on Tracy, Union forces in Cowan sent reinforcement under the command of Captain J. F. George of Company E, Second Massachusetts Infantry. They proceeded by railway to Tracy City, disembarking from the train a short distance from town. There, they threw out a skirmish line before proceeding cautiously into the town. Finding all quiet, they

---

[184] Ibid

returned to Cowan, but sent 2nd Lieutenant Gould and 43 men from the Third Maryland Volunteers to reinforce the command at Tracy City. Captain William W. Morse replaced Captain Upson as commander of the post.

In March of 1864, Hughes and Bledsoe were returning from a raid on Decherd where they destroyed a train. They stopped briefly in Beersheba Springs at the home of John Armfield to obtain grain for their horses. Hughes and his men descended the mountain and camped in a grove of trees near Mr. Dugan's house at the base of the opposite mountain.[185] About dawn the next day a band of Yankees under the command of General William B. Stokes rode into Beersheba brandishing pistols, in hot pursuit of the Rebels. There was said to be about three times as many as the 50 to 60 Rebels. Just after daybreak they surprised the rebel forces. Many of the men were still sleeping while others were preparing breakfast. Seven of Hughes men were reported killed and the rest escaped, leaving saddles, blankets, clothing, and arms. The rebels took off in the opposite direction, managing to

---

[185] Lucy Virginia French, pp. 38-39.
Location described is probably in Pepper Hollow near the foot of Tother Mountain.
[186] Ibid. 40.

scale the heights of the mountain on horseback and making a brief stand to prevent the Yankees from further pursuit. Hughes' personal papers, including his expense account, were lost.

One of the Rebels was reportedly shot after he surrendered. Mr. Dugan found his body and buried him. He was about 18 years old, and no one knew who he was or how to contact any of his relatives. A few days later two of the dead rebel's brothers showed up with a coffin and dug up his body and placed it in the coffin and buried him down in the valley with other victims that fell that day.[191]

William Dugan's story does not end there. Like many people during the war, Dugan tried to hide his valuables from bands of bushwhackers and foraging troops. Apparently, William asked his son John and a grandson to hide a large amount of gold and other valuables. After the war was over, they reported that the valuables had disappeared. William Dugan, perhaps understanding the amount of robbery and stealing in the area, may have attributed the disappearance to bands of robbers. However, upon his death in 1867, his heirs filed a lawsuit against John and the grandson, claiming they were responsible for the loss of the money, which should have been the inheritance of the plaintiffs. John and the grandson were eventually acquitted of any wrong doing, but hard feelings remained.[186]

Another incident left a lasting impression on the Goodman family in Pelham Valley and was recorded by George Goodman:

George Goodman of the 27th Tennessee Cavalry
Monday, March 9, 1908
I Was in Tennessee Army. I am a native of Tennessee; was born in Grundy County in 1845. I will be 63 years old March 28. I am one of those old ex-confederates, was in the Tennessee Army, Fourth Confederate Regiment, Company G. Barnes was our Captain.

He was a good officer and a good man.

I served awhile in Captain John P. Henley's Company. During my last service we ran some Tennessee Federals in a barn and they shot me through the right arm before we got them smoked out. I was in a fix then, sixty miles inside of their lines and not able to ride out. Next morning a boy by the name of Levan and I were carried up the side of Cumberland Mountain to an old still house and a man brought something to eat, and old man Levan and my mother found out where we were, and they come to us. The Federals had killed my Father; he was 53 years old when they killed him. He had been in the Army, but they

---

[186] Paul E. Sanders, *The Heritage of Grundy County TN 1844-2004*, (Walsworth Publishing Co. 2004), 178.

had discharged him. I had to hide 3 months in those mountains before I got to go in, and it was 12 months before I could use my right arm.

On the 25th of December 1864, a party of Confederate scouts made an attack on a band of Union Home Guards at the house of Sol. Goodman, in Grundy County, Tenn. The latter took refuge in a barn, to which the attacking party set fire, and so compelled their surrender. In the fight, George Goodman, of the Confederates, had his arm broken by a bullet. At that time, and under the circumstances, it was almost equivalent to death, for it was a conflict of neighbor against neighbor, and animosities were embittered and intensified by many bloody acts on each side, which called loudly for revenge. In this instance, Goodman's father (Anderson S. Goodman) had been brutally murdered by three of Brixey's men, who had formerly lived on his place and had often experienced his kindness. This act, of course, raised all of the devil in George's nature, and at every opportunity he made a raid into that section, and wreaked his vengeance upon his enemies. Now, that he was too badly wounded to make his way South to a place of safety, death truly stared him in the face as soon as his enemies should become aware of his defenseless condition. The news of his situation was borne to his widowed mother, and she at once realized its nature. As soon as possible she hastened to his assistance, determined to save him from the butchery which she knew would be his fate as soon as his whereabouts were made know.

Four miles from her house there was a high cliff of rocks, near the top of Cumberland Mountains, in a wild and unfrequented spot, and thither she contrived to get him without any one's help; for she feared the indiscretions of friends and a precious life, to her, hung on the event of concealment. The place was admirably suited for the purpose; the cliff jutted over, forming a roof, and some fallen rocks walled it in on one side. Waiting until midnight, she returned to her house four miles off, to get food and clothing. She knew that her absence and its object were known, and that her enemies would be on the lookout to discover George's whereabouts, so eager they were for his blood, and it can only be imagined with what caution she approached her own house, and what anxiety filled her breast until she secured what she wanted and was safely on her return. She had to cross Elk River on a log, but she said that she trusted Providence that it would not break under her until her journeying's were ended. For thirteen long weeks, in the middle of the unusually severe winter of '64-65, she returned every third night to her home for provisions, crossing and recrossing the frail bridge, until George was sufficiently recovered to take care of himself. It was but a short time after she ceased her travels that a party of Federals attempted to cross on the log that had borne the faithful old mother so long, when it broke and precipitated them into the river.

Such is a brief description of the mental tension this heroic woman had to undergo for more than three months. She thought, for a long time, that George would die, but she says she never lost hope. She had dreamed before the war that she would save him on that mountain, and would cover him with a certain quilt. So, when she started to his succor, she remembered her dream and took the quilt with her, and, in the darkest hours, in looking on it she felt her courage revive. Now she says it all seems like a dream- the occurrences that made up that age of suffering under the cliff. She prayed to God every step she took- prayed continually. She scarcely ate or slept, for George needed constant attention; the large nerve in his arm had been cut by the ball, and his suffering was acute and long continued, and his nervous system so shattered, in consequence, that he would scream out in terror at the slightest noise. Erysipelas also attacked his wound, and added to his danger; he was often delirious, and groaned continually. His mother says that one night, as she started off for food, she could hear him groan for a long distance, and could hardly hope that he would be alive on her return; but, when she approached the spot and heard his moaning, these evidences of life though tokens of great suffering, and were the sweetest sounds she ever heard.

Although it was the dead waste and middle of winter, she dared not build much fire, lest the smoke would be a cloud by day and the light a pillar of fire by night to guide her enemies to the spot. Nearly every day she could see them in the valley below, and frequently the light of a burning house; her own house was threatened, but she told her daughter to let it burn, and moved nothing out.

Wild cats were numerous on the mountain, and their savage screams at night added to the wildness and loneliness of her situation. The bleating of a flock of sheep, which came occasionally and rested on the mountain side, was of the greatest company to her, for it betokened no harm, and it was a blessed consolation, amid the warring elements surrounding her, to hear some sounds of innocence and peace.

Poor woman! As has been stated before, she scarcely ate or slept, and how she endured the mental strain of continual anxieties and fears, passes understanding. Faith, Hope, and Love all blended to give her strength, but the greatest of these was Love, which never once thought of bodily comfort, which halted before no danger nor sacrifice, but followed relentlessly as fate but one object- the saving of her darling boy.[187]

Grundy County would remain in Union hands for the rest of the war. Many Grundy County soldiers deserted when

---

[187] http://www.1stusinfantry.org/articles/bloodyTN.html

Bragg's army retreated across the Cumberland Mountains while others switched allegiances. A large number of Grundy County men were a part of the First Alabama and Tennessee Vidette Cavalry, which was formed in Stevenson Alabama. Many of the recruits were Confederate deserters from Grundy County. Many of the men enlisted at Tracy City, and one company was led by Stephen Tipton and Calvin Brixey.

"On July 6, [1863] Union General William Rosecrans sent out a circular noting that severe depredations of civilians were being committed by U. S. troops . . . Straggling soldiers had been committing outrages on citizens by robbing and thieving, quartermasters were taking forage improperly, and corps commanders were expected to crack down on both practices."[188]

Grundy County citizens were not safe in other parts of the state as well. In May of 1864, the *Nashville Dispatch* reported that Wm. Pearson of Grundy County had been shot on White's Creek Pike North of Nashville. The assailants were dressed as Union

---

[188] Michael Bradley. *Tullahoma: The 1863 Campaign for the Control of Middle Tennessee*, p.90.

soldiers and fired without provocation at Pearson, who was driving a wagon. Pearson died of his wounds.[189]

After Bledsoe's Raid on Tracy, there was little further military activity on the lower Cumberland Plateau. Tracy City also served as a supply base for the Union Army as they attempted to push the Confederate forces out of Chattanooga. The railroad line to Tracy City was repaired and food and ammunition flowed from the mountaintop to Union soldiers in and around Chattanooga. The supply line was threatened by Forrest's and Wheeler's cavalry, but for the most part, the raids had little lasting impact and the supply lines were kept open.

A detachment from the 89th Ohio under the command of Col. Caleb Carlton was sent to Tracy City to guard the supplies and protect the mines and railroad from guerilla attack. Later, the job of protecting Tracy City was assigned to Col. Stokes. Stokes also monitored University Place and Pelham Valley. It seems that some units remained camped in Pelham until early 1865.

Col. Edward Williams, of the Commissary department, wrote of his stay on the Cumberland Plateau at Sewanee. He

---

[189] *Nashville Dispatch*, May 23, 1864.

described the area as "one of the best camping grounds I know of . . . This place is so delightful and cool I hoped we might be permitted to spend the whole summer here."[190]

After the Tullahoma Campaign, Rosecrans rested his tired army while Bragg retreated to Chattanooga. In early September, Rosecrans moved forward, outflanked Bragg's army, and forced them out of Chattanooga. Bragg retreated south. The Union troops followed. Bragg received reinforcements led by General James Longstreet with nine brigades from Virginia. He launched a counterattack near Chickamauga Creek in northern Georgia. The attack drove the Union troops back toward Chattanooga. General George H. Thomas and his men made a determined stand, preventing a Confederate rout and allowed Rosecrans's army to limp back to Chattanooga. Thomas earned the nickname the "Rock of Chickamauga" for his actions there, and he subsequently replaced Rosecrans as Commander of the Union Army in the west.

Generals Longstreet and Nathan Bedford Forrest wanted to pursue the enemy. The Confederate Army had suffered some 20,000 casualties, including ten generals killed or wounded, and

---

[190] http://civilwar.gratzpa.org/2012/11/col-edward-c-williams-veteran-of-two-wars/

Bragg was reluctant to advance. Instead, he chose to lay siege on the Union Army in Chattanooga. In October, General Ulysses S. Grant arrived with reinforcements and drove the Confederates from the mountains around Chattanooga.

Bragg was replaced by General Joseph Johnston the following spring. Johnston's army retreated south, fighting a series of minor battles intended to prevent, or at least delay, the Union Army from reaching Atlanta, the main supply and communication center in the western theater still in Confederate control. General Johnston fought defensively. He entrenched his army in strategic positions across the path, forcing the Union armies into either a frontal assault or a flanking maneuver against well-prepared field troops. General William Tecumseh Sherman, leading the Union Army in the chase, often became frustrated and made tactical errors, but the dwindling Confederate Army was not strong enough to take advantage. Sherman tried a frontal assault at Kennesaw Mountain, some 20 miles northwest of Atlanta. The result was the loss of 3,000 men in a single day. The defeat at Kennesaw Mountain did not prevent Sherman's continued march toward Atlanta.

On June 14, 1864, at Pine Mountain, Generals Hardee, Johnston, and Polk were observing the Union Army from the top of the hill. General Sherman ordered his artillery to fire at the group over 600 yards away. As the officers began to retreat, one of the cannonballs hit General Polk who had stopped, some said, to pray, and killed him instantly. The loss was severely felt by the Confederate Army. While his generalship sometimes came into question, he was universally loved by his men. As Sam Watkins wrote: 'Every private soldier loved him."[191]

President Davis sent Braxton Bragg to Atlanta to evaluate the situation there. Bragg recommended that Johnston, the man that had replaced him, be replaced. Davis, who had a long feud with Johnston, turned command over to General John Bell Hood, who had lost a leg at Chickamauga. Hood, hyper and aggressive and suffering from the pain in his recently amputated leg, realized he had no chance to prevent Sherman from capturing Atlanta. After a series of attacks on Sherman's forces that had little effect, he abandoned Atlanta and marched north, hoping that Sherman's army would give chase.

---

[191] Sam Watkins, *Company Aytch*, 127.

Sherman ignored Hood and forced the surrender of Atlanta in September 1864. In doing so, he captured the remaining communication center in the South, boosting Northern morale and insuring President Abraham Lincoln's re-election in November.

Sherman ordered all manufacturing facilities in Atlanta burned. The fires got out of control, whether by accident or intention, and over a forth of Atlanta was destroyed while much of the remainder lay in ruins due to Union occupation.

Sherman then began what was called his March to the Sea. His troops laid waste to the countryside and resulted in the ultimate defeat of the South. Sherman headed toward Savannah, Georgia. The purpose of this March to the Sea was to destroy Southern morale and frighten the South into abandoning the Confederate cause. He said the North was "not only fighting hostile armies, but a hostile people, and must make old and young, rich and poor, feel the hard hand of war."[192]

Sherman's troops burned, stole, and destroyed much of a sixty-mile wide corridor in their path to Savannah. Their foragers

---

[192] William T. Sherman, in a letter to Major-General H. W. Halleck, Chief-of-Staff, Washington, D.C., December 24, 1864.

stole food and livestock and burned the houses and barns of people in their way. They arrived in Savannah on December 21, 1864. The city was undefended when they got there, and Sherman presented the city of Savannah to President Abraham Lincoln as a Christmas gift.

John Bell Hood continued to march north into Middle Tennessee as Sherman ravaged Georgia. Hood hoped to capture Nashville and force Sherman's withdrawal. Hood's piece-meal army encountered a well-entrenched Union Army in Franklin, Tennessee, some twenty miles south of Nashville. Ignoring recommendations from other officers to bypass the well-fortified army, or at least allow the cavalry to attack from the rear, Hood ordered a frontal assault. The result was a disaster. The Confederates lost over 6,000 men and six generals in the one-day battle.

The Union Army retreated to Nashville and Hood claimed a victory, but it was in reality the end of his Confederate Army in Tennessee. Hood followed the Union Army into Nashville but did not have the manpower to threaten the city. George H. Thomas, who had been sent to Nashville after Chickamauga, commanded the Union garrison there. On December 15, 1864,

Thomas's forces attacked and routed the weakened Confederate forces. Hood retreated to Franklin and south toward the Tennessee River. The weather was bitter cold, and snow had fallen. Many of the Confederate soldiers were barefoot, and most were without winter clothing. The Union troops followed in hot pursuit for ten days. General Nathan Bedford Forrest and his men served as rear guard, the only thing protecting the Army of Tennessee from destruction. They crossed the Tennessee River on December 26th and the Union Army halted pursuit. The Army of Tennessee would never again be a fighting force.

The story of Dr. John Farris illustrated the dangers facing citizens in the Grundy County area near the end of the war. John K. Farris was a medical doctor who was treating wounded men at Franklin when the Southern Army retreated from Nashville. He was captured by Union forces and told to report with the wounded men in his care to Nashville. Dr. Farris, George Martin from Franklin County, and a soldier named Moore from East Tennessee managed to escape and after eight days and nights, reached Farris's home near Hillsboro, Tennessee. The weather was freezing, and he had to elude pickets and Home Guard on his way back to Coffee County. Farris stopped by his house to get some warmer clothing and tried to determine where the Confederate Army was now located. He traveled through Pelham, skirting the Union troops stationed there, and crossed the mountain in an attempt to rejoin his regiment. When he reached the Tennessee River, he found every avenue of crossing closed, and he returned to his home near Hillsboro.

Upon returning home, he found bands of guerillas were making life difficult there. "My community was infested by the murderous gang of Brixey's men who were killing and burning in the neighborhood. I was a practicing physician and my neighbors very much wanted and needed my services . . . . There was very much bitterness on the part of the Brixey gang."[193]

Finding no way to escape the harassment of the Brixietes, as Brixey's men were known in the area, Dr. Farris sought protection from the Federal Provost Marshal in Decherd. The Provost Marshal promised protection but required Dr. Farris to make the 28 mile round-trip once a week to check in with him at his headquarters. The doctor borrowed a horse and began

---

[193] John K. Farris, Letters to Mary: The Civil War Diary of John Kennerly Farris, Franklin County Historical Review. Vol. XXV, 1994. pp. 139-140.

making rounds in the neighboring areas, but never totally escaped the danger of Brixey and his men.

Things were not going any better for the Army of Northern Virginia. From the time of the defeat at Gettysburg, Robert E. Lee's Army of Northern Virginia had been a beaten foe. They abandoned Richmond, the Confederate capital in the spring of 1865. Union forces under the command of U.S. Grant greatly outnumbered the bedraggled Confederate troops. Union forces had cut off Lee's attempted retreat to North Carolina, and he was forced to surrender. The official surrender took place in the tiny town of Appomattox Courthouse, Virginia on April 9th, 1865. Though sporadic fighting continued for several days, the war was officially over.

General Nathan Bedford Forrest addressed his troops in May of 1865 to inform them of the surrender of the Confederate forces. His men were loyal and likely to follow his lead.

He chose his words carefully:

By an agreement made between Liet.-Gen. Taylor, commanding the Department of Alabama. Mississippi, and East Louisiana, and Major-Gen. Canby, commanding United States forces, the troops of this department have been surrendered.

I do not think it proper or necessary at this time to refer to causes which have reduced us to this extremity; nor is it now a matter of material consequence to us how such results were brought about. That we are BEATEN is a self-evident fact, and any further resistance on our part would justly be regarded as the very height of folly and rashness.

The armies of Generals LEE and JOHNSON having surrendered. You are the last of all the troops of the Confederate States Army east of the Mississippi River to lay down your arms.

The Cause for which you have so long and so manfully struggled, and for which you have braved dangers, endured privations, and sufferings, and made so many sacrifices, is today hopeless. The government which we sought to establish and perpetuate, is at an end. Reason dictates and humanity demands that no more blood be shed. Fully realizing and feeling that such is the case, it is your duty and mine to lay down our arms – submit to the "powers that be" – and to aid in restoring peace and establishing law and order throughout the land.

The terms upon which you were surrendered are favorable and should be satisfactory and acceptable to all. They manifest a spirit of magnanimity and liberality, on the part of the Federal authorities, which should be met, on our part, by a faithful compliance with all the stipulations and conditions therein expressed. As your Commander, I sincerely hope that every officer and soldier of my command will cheerfully obey the orders given and carry out in good faith all the terms of the cartel.

Those who neglect the terms and refuse to be paroled, may assuredly expect, when arrested, to be sent North and imprisoned. Let those who are absent from their commands, from whatever cause, report at once to this place, or to Jackson, Miss.; or, if too remote from either, to the nearest United States post or garrison, for parole.

Civil war, such as you have just passed through naturally engenders feelings of animosity, hatred, and revenge. It is our duty to divest ourselves of all such feelings; and as far as it is in our power to do so, to cultivate friendly feelings towards those with whom we have so long contended, and heretofore so widely, but honestly, differed. Neighborhood feuds, personal animosities, and private differences should be blotted out; and, when you return home, a manly, straightforward course of conduct will secure the respect of your enemies. Whatever your responsibilities may be to Government, to society, or to individuals meet them like men.

The attempt made to establish a separate and independent Confederation has failed; but the consciousness of having done your duty faithfully, and to the end, will, in some measure, repay for the hardships you have undergone.

In bidding you farewell, rest assured that you carry with you my best wishes for your future welfare and happiness. Without, in any way, referring to the merits of the Cause in which we have been engaged, your courage and determination, as exhibited on many hard-fought fields, has elicited the respect and admiration of friend and foe. And I now cheerfully and gratefully acknowledge my indebtedness to the officers and men of my command whose zeal, fidelity and unflinching bravery have been the great source of my past success in arms.

I have never, on the field of battle, sent you where I was unwilling to go myself; nor would I now advise you to a course which I felt myself unwilling to pursue. You have been good soldiers, you can be good citizens.

Obey the laws, preserve your honor, and the Government to which you have surrendered can afford to be, and will be, magnanimous.

N.B. Forrest, Lieut.-General
Headquarters, Forrest's Cavalry Corps
Gainesville, Alabama
May 9, 1865[194]

---

[194] https://civilwartalk.com/threads/gen-nathan-bedford-forrest-sends-his-men-home-150-yearsago.113338/

Aftermath

On the evening of April 14, 1865, Abraham Lincoln attended a special performance of the comedy, *Our American Cousin*. President Lincoln was accompanied to Ford's Theater in Washington, D.C. by his wife, Mary Todd Lincoln, a twenty-eight-year-old officer named Major Henry R. Rathbone, and Rathbone's fiancée, Clara Harris. Actor John Wilkes Booth, who was a national figure and southern sympathizer, slipped into Lincoln's presidential box and fired his .50 caliber derringer pistol into the back of Lincoln's head.

Rathbone lunged at Booth. Booth slashed his arm with a dagger and jumped over the railing to the stage below. As Booth leapt from the balcony, he caught the spur of his left boot on a flag draped over the rail and shattered a bone in his leg on landing. Though injured, he rushed out the back door, climbed on an awaiting horse and rode calmly across the river into Maryland. A doctor in the audience immediately went upstairs to the box. The assassin's bullet had entered through Lincoln's left ear and lodged behind his right eye. He was paralyzed and barely breathing. Lincoln was carried across Tenth Street to a boardinghouse opposite the theater, but the doctors' best efforts failed. At 7:22 AM on April 15th, Lincoln died.

Booth was the leader of a larger conspiracy to paralyze the Union government by assassinating Lincoln, Vice-President Andrew Johnson and Secretary of State William Seward. About the same time that Booth fired his fatal shot, two of his accomplices, Lewis Powell and David Herold, approached the Washington home of Secretary of State William Henry Seward. The Secretary had been bedridden since a carriage accident.

Powell knocked on the door of Seward's home as Herold waited outside. Lewis Powell forced his way inside and attacked Seward, stabbing him several times, but Seward miraculously survived. The assassin who was assigned to kill Johnson failed to follow through.

David Herold fled the bloody scene at Seward's house, leaving Powell behind and soon caught up with Booth in the Maryland countryside. The two rode to a tavern owned by Mary Surratt in Surrattsville, Maryland (Now Clinton) where the two fugitives collected some previously stashed supplies. They then rode to the house of Dr. Samuel Mudd, arriving early the next morning. Booth was in extreme pain and asked Dr. Mudd for help. Mudd hesitantly let them in and later testified that even though he was acquainted with Booth, he did not recognize him as he set his leg. Mudd also arranged for carpenter John Bess to make Booth a pair of crutches.

The next day, Booth and Herold made their way through Zekiah Swamp, a twenty-one-mile strip of slush and bogs that are part of the Wicomico River, with the help of a black tobacco farmer, to the home of Samuel Cox, a Confederate sympathizer. Cox directed them to a hiding place and sent for Thomas A. Jones, a Confederate agent. Federal troops were combing the countryside and Jones advised them to remain where they were—outdoors in a thicket of pine trees—until it was safe to cross the Potomac to Virginia. During their five-day wait, most of their accomplices in the assassination were rounded up.

Booth's first attempt to cross the Potomac was unsuccessful, but on April 22, they managed to cross the river into Virginia. There, they were helped by some Confederate soldiers and ended up at Richard Garrett's farm near Bowling Green, Virginia.

Having questioned the Confederate soldiers that helped Booth and finding out where they were hiding, the 16th New York Cavalry arrived at the Garrett farm at 2 o'clock on the morning of

April 26th. Herold and Booth were concealed in the barn. The Garrets had locked the barn, and the fugitives were unable to escape. They were ordered to surrender, which Herold did, but Booth remained inside. The soldiers piled straw against the barn and set it on fire. The fire spread throughout the structure, but Booth still refused to surrender. Sergeant Boston Corbett fired his rifle through a crack in the barn, mortally wounding Booth who was paralyzed and died later that morning.

The remaining conspirators were rounded up, except for Confederate spy John Surratt, Mary Surratt's son, who escaped to Europe. George Azterodt, who was assigned to kill Vice President Andrew Johnson, but lost his nerve and stayed in a hotel bar, drinking; Lewis Powell who attempted to murder Secretary of State; Mary Surratt, who owned the boarding house where the conspirators met; and David Herold, who had accompanied Booth on his attempted escape were all hanged at Old Arsenal Penitentiary in Washington, D.C. on July 7th 1865. Dr. Samuel Mudd, who had treated Booth's leg, was sentenced to life in prison, as were two friends of Booth who appeared to have little or no connection to the conspiracy, Michael O'Laughlen and Samuel Arnold.

Over the next several months, a straggling procession of grey-clad, gaunt, hungry, ragged and crippled men slowly made their way home. For the most part, they traveled on foot, often in groups of two or three, surviving on handouts from local people. In many areas, the travel was dangerous, as Home Guards and other bushwhackers used the opportunity to settle old scores.

The countryside through which they traveled was in ruin. Houses and barns had been burned, fences torn down and used for firewood, and most of the animals and food stolen. In many cases, only chimneys remained where houses had stood. Families were often starving and had nothing to give to the hungry stragglers who knocked at their doors almost daily.

The war had a devastating effect on Grundy County as it did on the rest of the South. Union and Confederate Armies had stripped the countryside of everything of value.

Once prosperous farms where now barren of crops. In every category, Grundy County's 300 farms were far less prosperous in 1870 than they had been in 1860. Few farms had produced anywhere near the numbers of crop they had prior to the war. There was a shortage of animals. Slaves were free and no longer available to work the land, and the entire countryside was in disarray.

Adrian Northcutt would die in 1869. Northcutt's family, who avoided the worst depredations of the foraging armies because their location in Northcutt's Cove was off the beaten path, still lost 100 improved acres and 1,000 unimproved acres in the decade of the Civil War. Alexander Patton would die in 1879, his holdings greatly reduced from the 1860 census. Coincidentally, Patton's neighbor, Solomon P. Goodman, whose farm in 1860 had had a cash value second only to Patton's own, also died in 1879, leaving more debts than assets in his estate.[195]

---

[195] http://grundycountyhistory.org/05_Res/Census/Grundy%20Special%20Census.pdf, p. XI.

[202] Letter from V. L. Northcutt to Tom Russell. Nov. 29, 1976. Shared with Author by Bettye Sherwood.

What happened to the African American population in Grundy County after 1865? A letter written by V. L. Northcutt, a grandson of Adrian Northcutt, sheds some light on the fate of the slaves. He writes that "all the slaves of Cope {His other grandfather James Cope} and Gen Adrian stayed with their masters. Cope had thousands of acres of land and gave every acre of his land to his slaves."[202]

While this may not be entirely accurate, it is likely that the slaves for the most part remained in the local area, at least for the immediate future. By 1870, the landscape had changed. Most of those freed slaves left the county before 1870. The population of free blacks and slaves in 1860 was 280, but in 1870 there were only 137 black persons in the county. This indicates a loss of roughly half the black population. Familiar surroundings and local knowledge would have been valuable assets for the newly emancipated slaves.

The largest concentration of black residents lived in the Hubbard's Cove area, or civil district I. Their surnames on the population schedules indicate that most of them were descendants of the Wooten, Winton and Guest slaves who populated that area in 1850 and 1860.[196]

One slave, Georgia Patton Washington, who was born on Alexander Patton's plantation in Pelham, became the 1st African American doctor in Tennessee. Patton's slave quarters were located on the hill at the end of Wilson-Allen Road in Pelham.

After the war, Georgia's mother moved to nearby Coffee County where she worked as a seamstress. Georgia was a bright and inquisitive girl and managed to complete high school despite the lack of educational opportunities for African-Americans. Her family mustered together enough money to send her to Central Tennessee College in Nashville, TN. Through hard work and determination, she finished college and enrolled at Meharry Medical School where she graduated in 1893. At the time she was only the third woman to have graduated from Meharry. She traveled to Liberia where she worked for years as a medical missionary. When she returned to the states, she settled in Memphis, TN where she became the first African-American woman in Tennessee to receive both her physician's and surgeon's license.[197]

---

[196]http://grundycountyhistory.org/05_Res/Census/Grundy%20Special%20Census.pdf, p. X.

Like most of Tennessee and much of the South, Grundy County was ravaged by the Civil War. It would take many years to recoup the losses. Perhaps Abraham Lincoln summed up the feelings of most Americans when he said, "There is no honorable way to kill, no gentle way to destroy. There is nothing good in war except its ending."

---

[197] http://www.blackpast.org/aah/patton-georgia-e-l-1864-1900.

Appendix

I have not attempted to conceal any of the peculiarities or defects of the Southern people. Many persons will doubtless highly disapprove of some of their customs and habits in the wilder portion of the country; but I think no generous man, whatever may be his political opinions, can do otherwise than admire the courage, energy, and patriotism of the whole population, and the skill of its leaders, in this struggle against great odds. And I am also of opinion that many will agree with me in thinking that a people in which all ranks and both sexes display a unanimity and a heroism which can never have been surpassed in the history of the world.

James Arthur Fremantle

http://docsouth.unc.edu/imls/fremantle/fremantle.html P. 3

Civil War Quotes

"It is well that war is so terrible, or we would grow too fond of it." -
Robert E. Lee

"Let us cross over the river and rest under the shade of the trees."

- Last words of **Thomas "Stonewall" Jackson**

"We have but one flag, one country; let us stand together. We may differ in color, but not in sentiment. Many things have been said about me which are wrong, and which white and black persons here, who stood by me through the war, can contradict. Go to work, be industrious, live honestly and act truly, and when you are oppressed I'll come to your relief."

-Nathan Bedford Forrest

ACTS OF TENNESSEE 1843-44, CHAPTER 204:

"AN ACT TO ESTABLISH THE COUNTY OF GRUNDY."

SECTION 1. BE IT ENACTED BY THE GENERAL ASSEMBLY OF THE STATE OF TENNESSEE, That a new county be, and the same is hereby established, by taking a part of the counties of Warren and Coffee, to be known and designated by the name of Grundy, in honor of the Honorable Felix Grundy, deceased.

SECTION 2. BE IT ENACTED, That the beginning corner of the county of Grundy shall commence in the center of the stage road leading from McMinnville, where the Coffee County line crosses the same; thence a southerly direction, so as not to approach Manchester nearer than twelve miles, until near Benjamin Douglas'; thence eastwardly up the mountain to the top; thence with the meanders of the bluffs to the line of District No. 13, in Coffee County; thence with said line to the line of Franklin County; thence east with said line to James Petty's, near the foot of Cumberland Mountain; thence with the burned stand road to the line of Marion County; thence with said line to the line of Warren County; thence with the line of Warren County, to the line of Van Buren County; thence west with said line to the corner of Jesse Savage's; thence round the Bluffs of Hill's Creek, so as not to approach nearer the town of McMinnville than twelve miles, to a point on the road leading to the Bershebee [sic] Springs, twelve miles south-east from McMinnville; thence westwardly crossing the mountains, so as to keep twelve miles from McMinnville, to a point near Jesse Fults; thence westwardly passing between John Brown Esq., and William Roton's; thence a direct line to the beginning; said lines in no case to approach nearer than twelve miles of the town of McMinnville and Manchester.

SECTION 3. For the purpose of organizing the county of Grundy, William Dugan, Adrian Northcut, and James Tate, from the county of Warren, and Alfred Brawley and John Burrows, of the county of Coffee, shall be and are hereby appointed commissioners, who shall take an oath before some justice of the peace, faithfully and impartially to discharge the duties enjoined upon them in this act, and in all cases of vacancy that may occur among said commissioners previous to the organization of the county court of Grundy County, the same shall be filled by the other commissioners, and all cases occurring after the said organization, shall be filled by the county court of Grundy County, the said commissioners shall enter into bond and security, to be approved by the county court of Grundy County, and payable to the Chairman thereof, in the sum of two thousand dollars, conditioned for the faithful discharge of their several duties; a majority of said commissioners shall constitute a board to do all things herein enjoined upon them, they shall keep a regular record of all their proceedings as commissioners, which shall be returned to the county court of Grundy County at their first session, and the same shall be recorded by the clerk thereof, on the records of said court, and they shall make such other returns after the organization of said court, as shall be directed thereby.

SECTION 4. It shall be the duty of said commissioners, first giving ten days notice, in two or more public places, of the time and places to open and hold an election at one or more places in each of the fractions proposed to be stricken off from the counties of Warren and Coffee, respectively, for the purpose of ascertaining whether a majority of the voters residing in the several fractions are in favor of, or opposed to the establishment of the county of Grundy, and all persons qualified to vote for members of the General Assembly, who have resided in the fractions proposed to be stricken off, six months immediately preceding the day of election, shall be entitled to vote, and each voter who desires to vote for the establishment of the new county, shall have on his ticket the words "new county," and those voting against the new county shall have on their tickets the words "old county", and if upon counting all the ballots, the judges of several fractions shall return that a majority of each of the fractions have voted for the new county, then the county of Grundy shall be, and the same is hereby established with all the powers, privileges and advantages, and subject to all the liabilities and duties with other counties in this state.

SECTION 5. That for the due administration of justice, the different courts to be held in said county of Grundy, shall be held at Beersheba Springs until the seat of justice shall be established, that the County Court shall in the intermediate time, have full power to adjourn the courts to such other place in said county as they deem better suited for the same, and for public convenience, and to adjourn to the seat of justice when in their judgment the necessary arrangements are made; and all writs and other precepts issuing from any of said courts returnable to either place shall and may be returned to the place to which said court may have been removed by the county court aforesaid, and the courts of the county of Grundy shall be under the same rules, regulations, and restrictions, and shall have, hold, exercise and possess the same powers and jurisdiction as are prescribed by law for holding courts in other counties; said county shall be attached to the 13th Judicial Circuit, and the circuit courts shall be held by the judge of said circuit, on the second Mondays in April, August, and December in each and every year, and the citizens of said county may file bills in chancery, at the Chancery Court at McMinnville.

SECTION 6. All officers civil and military in said county, shall continue to hold their offices and exercise all the powers and functions thereof, until others are elected according to law; and the said county of Grundy shall elect her officers on the same day, and under the same regulations as provided by law for the election of officers in other counties in this state; PROVIDED, that nothing in this act contained shall deprive the above named counties from having, holding, and exercising jurisdiction over the territory composing the county of Grundy and the citizens thereof in as full and ample a manner as they now have, until the election of county officers takes place according to law; PROVIDED ALSO, nothing herein shall prevent the above named counties from rendering judgments, or the sheriffs of said counties from selling under such judgments any lands within the bounds of said county of Grundy, for taxes, costs, and charges, until the county of Grundy shall be fully organized.

SECTION 7. The citizens of Grundy County in all elections for Governor, Representatives in Congress, members of the General Assembly, and Electors of President and Vice President, shall vote with the counties from which they have been respectively stricken off, until the next apportionment agreeable to the fifth section of the tenth article of the constitution of Tennessee.

SECTION 8. It shall be the duty of the commissioners aforesaid, as soon after the county of Grundy shall have been established as practicable, to select and procure by purchase or otherwise a suitable site for the seat of justice in said county, having due regard to the convenience and wishes of a majority of the citizens of said county, and the said commissioners having first caused a deed to be made to themselves and their successors with general warranty, to a sufficient quantity of land including the site so selected, shall cause a town to be laid off thereon, with as many streets of such width as they may deem necessary, reserving a sufficient quantity of land for a public square; said commissioners shall designate and reserve from sale one lot in said tow on which to build a public jail for said county, and also such other lots as they may deem prudent, on which to erect other public or religious buildings; said town so laid off shall be known by such name as said commissioners may give it.

SECTION 9. That the commissioners of said county shall sell the lots in said town, on a credit of at least twelve months, first giving due notice thereof in one or more newspapers, and shall take bond with sufficient security from the purchasers of said lots, payable to themselves, and their successors in office, and shall make title in fee simple as commissioners to the respective purchasers of said lots.

SECTION 10. The proceeds of the sale of the lots aforesaid shall be a fund in the hands of the commissioners for defraying the expenses incurred in the purchase of said tract of land, on which said seat of Justice shall be located and also for defraying the expenses of erecting the public buildings for said county of Grundy.

SECTION 11. The commissioners shall superintend the building of such public buildings as the county court of said county shall order and direct to be built, (and shall order and direct to be built) and shall let the same out and take bonds from the undertakers with ample penalties and securities payable to themselves and their successors, conditioned for the faithful performance of his or their contracts, that the balance if any, of the proceeds arising from the sales of the lots of said town remaining in the hands of said commissioners after defraying the expenses aforesaid shall be paid over by said commissioners to the trustee of said county of Grundy, to be held, applied, and accounted for by him as other county funds.

SECTION 12. The said commissioners shall appoint five suitable persons as commissioners whose duty it shall be to divide and lay off said county of Grundy into civil districts, designate the place for holding elections therein, and do and perform all the duties relative thereto which by the laws of this state such commissioners are authorized and required to do.

SECTION 13. The county of Grundy shall form one regiment, which shall be known and designated as the 161st regiment, and shall be attached to the tenth brigade. The militia officer or officers highest in command included within said county of Grundy, shall at such time and place as he or they may determine upon, call all the commissioned officers together, and such of them as shall attend, are hereby authorized and empowered to lay off said county into battalions and companies and provide for holding elections for the purpose of electing all officers in said regiment in the manner prescribed by law.

SECTION 14. The county court shall be and is hereby authorized to make such allowance as they may deem reasonable as a compensation to said county commissioners for their services in organizing said county, to be paid out of the treasury of said county of Grundy.

SECTION 15. BE IT ENACTED, That to avoid all litigation, cost and dispute which may arise in settling the boundaries of said county of Grundy, and to secure the counties of Coffee and Warren from being reduced below their constitutional limits, it shall be the duty of the commissioners appointed by the third section of this act, previous to the holding of the election provided for in the fourth section of this act, to cause to be made a re-survey of all the boundary lines of said counties, and that they shall give notice to the county court of Coffee County, of the time when the line will be run taking off so much of the territory as is taken from said county of Coffee, and also notice to the county court of Warren, of the time when the line will be run taking off a portion of said county of Warren, which notices shall be given sixty days before the running of said line, and shall be given by a written notice by said commissioners or a majority of them, directed to the county court and filed with the clerk of the same, and the said courts shall have power, and may at their discretion, respectively appoint a commissioner or surveyor to superintend on the part of each of said counties, the making of the several surveys, so far as each county is concerned, to see that the limits of each of said counties of Warren and Coffee, are not reduced below their proper constitutional limits; each of said commissioners or surveyors so appointed by said county courts, to act on behalf of the county and county court within which he has been appointed, and if said courts shall refuse or decline to make such appointment, after such notice, the said commissioners mentioned in the said third section, may proceed to make said re-survey, and lay off by running the lines described in this act, and shall, when said survey is completed, so as to include the proper constitutional limits in said county, and not reducing the said other counties below their constitutional limits, and shall cause said survey to be recorded and registered in the Register's office of said county of Grundy when the same is organized, and said boundaries shall become so established, and when marked and designated by the general calls contained in this act; and the re-survey here provided for, shall be made by a sworn surveyor, and sworn chain carriers, under direction of said commissioners named in the third section,

and such as may be appointed by said county courts; PROVIDED, that nothing in this act contained, shall be so construed as to authorize or attach any portion of the territory now belonging to Marion County, to the county of Grundy.

PASSED ON JANUARY 29, 1844

Signers of the 1843 Petition

- Northcut, Adrain
- Northcut, John
- Tate Sr., John
- Tate Jr., Tate
- Tate, Major Eliuson
- Wilkerson, John
- Brown, Thomas
- Brown, Dial
- Nunley, Greenberry
- King, Thomas
- Gross, Andrew
- Tate, John G.
- King, Stokes
- King, John
- King, Lacy
- Tate Sr., James
- Tate, Elon
- Tate Jr., James
- Perry, Henry
- Perry Sr., John
- Brown Sr., Thomas
- Perry Sr., William
- Perry, Samuel
- Perry, Stephen
- Perry Jr., John
- Perry Jr., William
- Tate Sr., Robert
- Tate, Aaron
- Prince, John
- Coppinger, Jesse
- Coppinger, Alex
- Coppinger, David
- Nunly Jr., Jeremiah
- Henshaw, William
- Northcut, Stephen
- Northcut Jr., James
- Nunley, Wm. B.
- Henson, Moses
- Nunley, Levi
- collins, Jacob
- Patrick, John
- Clay, Joseph
- Countis, Peter
- Countis, Henderson
- Countis, William
- Bost, Noah
- Howell, Price
- Levan, Henderson
- Levan, Thompson
- Levan, John
- Killian, Ambrose
- Walker, Jeremiah
- Walker Jr., Jeremiah
- Jones, Abraham
- Jones, Robert
- Jones, Harris
- Step, Rich.
- Walker, James
- Walker, James
- Walker Jr., John
- Walker Sr., John
- Walker, William
- Gross, Lawson
- Levan, Henry
- Walker, Zedekiah
- Levan, James
- Walker, Elijah
- Daubey, John
- Oliver, Ahepah
- Oliver, Richard
- Nunley, Jesse
- Lockhart, James
- Lockhart Sr., John
- Lockhart Jr., John
- Lockhart, Robert
- Housholder, Thomas
- Rogers, Carrole
- Gross Sr., John
- Gross, Samuel
- Gross Jr., John
- Gross, William
- Gross, Asa
- Dykes, Isham
- Prince, Greenbury
- Bond Sr., Wm.
- Bond, Wilson
- Bond, Walker
- Rogers, P. H.
- Vicars, James
- Rogers, Terrell
- Dugan Sr., Wm.20
- Dugan, Robert

Dugan, John
Ransom, Parkal
Wilson, Ballard
Ransom, Washington
Lockhart, James
Dugan Jr., William
Dykes Sr., John
Bowlin, _____
Savage, Warren
Savage, _____
Savage Sr., Sterling
Cagle, Christopher
Cagle, Charles
Cagle, John
Fults, Jesse
Stoner, Henry
Stoner, William
Stoner, Wilson
Nunley Sr., Wm.
Nunley, Ellis
Nunley, John
Hobbs Sr., Ezekiel
D_____, C_____
Dykes, Martin
Dykes, Saunder
Oliver, R. H.
Savage, Jesse
Savage, Simeon
Hunter, Squire
Cuningham, John
Spong, Henry T.
Campbell, Isaac
Campbell, William
Stringer, James
Thompson, David

Nunley Sr., Jeremiah
Nunley, William R.
Nunley, Davidson
Nunley, Archebald
Davis, James
Davis, William
Fults, Smith
Sudin?, Robert
Gibbs, James
Gibbs, John
Gibbs, Ezekiel
Gibbs, Isaac
Saunders, James
Tate, Robert
Lane, Daniel
Sitz, Wm.
Bailey, Thomas
Thompson, John
Thompson, Wm.
Ricketts, George
Ricketts, Thomas
Ricketts, James
Ricketts, Peter
Tate, Alex
Cagle Sr., Jacob
Cagle, Henry
Cagle Sr., Jacob
Dunaway, Wm.20
Dunaway, John
Dunaway, James
Dunaway, George
Samples, George
Samples, Martin

Sweeden, Jackson
Sweeden, Caroll
Hobbs, Christopher
Hobbs, Richard
Hobbs, Adreen
Hobbs, James
Hobbs Jr., Ezekiel
Scott, Jonathan
Scott, Pleasant
Scott, Edward
Smartt, Jospeh
Smartt, John
Smartt, Reubin
Smartt, Wm.
Green, Samuel
Green, Shadrack
Green, Wm.
Green, Davidson
Martin, Thomas
Anglin, John
Freeze, James
Tipton, Jonathan
Fults, Anderson
Tipton, John
McGee, John
Armstrong, Wm.
Cowen, Samuel
Miller, Greenberry
Wooten, Wm.
Wootton, Jackson
Meadows, Hale
Quawls, Samuel
Adams, Martin
Campbell, Wm.
Campbell Sr., James

Campbell, Duncan	Myres, Christopher	Pearson, Starlin20
Campbell, Riley	Myres, John	Crabtree, Jonson
Campbell, James	Myres Jr., Casper	Wooton, Jesse
Campbell, John	N_____	Rhea, Joseph against it
Campbell, Enock	Willison?, David	Wooten, Jesse
Fults, Lilbourn	_____, Smith	Wooten, Mikiel
Campbell, Archebald	Wilkerson, _____	Martin, Thomas
Dickerson, William	Wilkerson, Col.	Guest, Wm.
Lowe, Leonard	Cuts?, Ekgah	Lusk, John
Lowe, Hugh	Meeks, James	Lusk, Squire
Myres, Jacob	Roberts, Benjamin	Hetton, Wyatt
Myres Sr., Casper	Phillips, Ephraim	Hoover, Abraham
Cocks, David	Meeks, John	Coulson, James
Meeks, Isaac	Gibbs, George	Smith, Washington
Sanders, Silas	Sumers, Basil	James, Joseph
Sanders, Euray C.	Price, Morgan	Landreth, James
Sanders, Thomas	Moore, Isaac	Braley, Greek
Hanes?, Daniel	Roberts Sr., Isaac	Braley, J_____
Myres, Griffin	_____, George	Braley, Thomas
Myres, Pleasant	Warren, John	Guest, Moses against the petition
Fults Sr., John	_____, Mill	Lusk, William L.
Fults Jr., Adam	Sumer, George W.	Cungham, Bew_____
Crouch, Wm.	Lowe, Charles F.	Braley Esq., Alfred against
Fults, Pleasant	Lowe, William	Wooton, A.
Kelton, William	Turner, John	Berry, Green
Kelton, James	Summers, John	Braley Jr., Leroy against
Kelton, Pleasant	King, John	Southorland, Samuel
Kelton, Robert	Lowe, John L.	Park, William
Kelton, Wilson	Roberts, Silas T.	Cornelison, Jesse
Scott, Jefferson	Todd, Davidson	Fults, Daniel
Scott, J. K.	Coap, Steahen	Fults, Alfred
Scott, Thomas	Tucker, Samuel	
Lowe, Ezekiel		
Lowe, William		

Cates, Elijah	Braley Jr., Alfred20
Dickerson, Archibald	Braley Jr., John
Adams, Laz	_____, Samuel
Tompson, William	Wooten, James
Tompson, Archelous	____, William
Nonley, Amanuel	Braley, Col. against
Noneley, Hiram	Braley, John against
Struges, James	Berry, Wm.
Fults, Smith	Wilson, Benjamin against
Sides, Wm.	
Dickerson, William H.	Braley, Samuel against
R_tenger, Wm.	Braley, Walter against
Cope, William	Sain, D. in favor of
Roberts, William	Paxton, Mordica in favor of
Cocke, Nathan	
Pearson, Eller	Scott, William
Pearson, S____ C.	Moonry, W. S. [opposed to be included in the county only]
Darden, Robert	
Martin, Erns S.	Lan___, James in favor
Gilles, John against it	Campbell, William
Leven/Lawson, William	Landers, Hardon in favor
____, Fedore	
Martin, Edmond	Sain, Thomas in favor of
Meadows, Hale	
Winton, James	Adams, Harrison in favor
Moore, Joseph	Hany, Ely
Hooer, John M.	
Coulson, Bartlet	
Coulson, Alex	
Martin, Peter	
Paxton, Mordica	
Coulson, Joseph	
Angen, Wm.	

Index

A

Abraham Lincoln, **8**, **9**, **35**, **36**, **37**, **39**, **42**, **46**, **55**, **134**, **192**, **193**, **236**, **237**, **245**, **253**

Ainsworth, **210**, **213**

Alabama-Tennessee Vidette Cavalry, **187**, **197**

Albin Schoepf, **119**, **122**

Alexander Patton, **57**, **69**, **94**, **98**, **99**, **198**, **250**, **252**

Altamont, **62**, **75**, **79**, **80**, **81**, **82**, **83**, **84**, **89**, **91**, **114**, **116**, **117**, **118**, **119**, **120**, **121**, **123**, **179**, **180**, **197**, **208**, **211**, **215**, **219**, **222**

Anderson, **52**, **149**, **196**, **204**, **206**, **227**, **262**

Andrew Jackson Phipps, **190**

Andrew Lytle, **2**, **135**, **157**

Atlanta, **136**, **183**, **234**, **235**, **236**

B

Benjamin Magee, **148**, **150**

Big Creek, **121**

Blackmore, **213**, **214**

Bledsoe, **50**, **217**, **218**, **219**, **220**, **222**, **223**, **224**, **232**

Boiling Fork Creek, **158**

Booth, **245**, **246**, **247**, **248**

Bragg, **18**, **45**, **112**, **116**, **117**, **119**, **120**, **126**, **127**, **130**, **131**, **132**, **136**, **138**, **139**, **140**, **142**, **143**, **144**, **145**, **146**, **150**, **151**, **154**, **155**, **156**, **159**, **166**, **167**, **169**, **170**, **171**, **173**, **195**, **217**, **231**, **233**, **234**, **235**

Brake-field Point, **148**

Brasher, **216**

Bridgeport, **60**, **162**, **186**

Brixey, **4**, **180**, **184**, **186**, **187**, **194**, **196**, **197**, **200**, **201**, **204**, **205**, **206**, **207**, **208**, **209**, **227**, **231**, **239**

Burnett, **191**, **197**, **198**

C

Cal Brixey, **196**

Coffee County, **62**, **65**, **70**, **94**, **186**, **200**, **206**,

238, 252, 256, 259

Col. W. B. Stokes, **182**

Collins, **64**, **71**

Colonel John Wilder, **144**

Conatzy, **204**, **205**, **206**

Cowan, **87**, **114**, **148**, **155**, **156**, **157**, **158**, **164**, **166**, **222**, **223**

Cumberland Mountains, **131**, **141**, **148**, **170**, **197**, **228**, **231**

Cumberland Plateau, **50**, **58**, **62**, **64**, **88**, **140**, **155**, **163**, **164**, **176**, **232**

D

Decherd, **62**, **145**, **146**, **149**, **151**, **152**, **165**, **166**, **167**, **174**, **206**, **224**, **239**

Don Carlos Buell, **106**, **117**, **121**, **132**

Dred Scott, **32**, **33**, **35**

Duck River, **65**, **128**

Dugan, **72**, **73**, **90**, **224**, **225**, **256**, **261**, **262**

E

Edmund Kirby Smith, **117**, **142**

Elk River, **64**, **65**, **66**, **68**, **69**, **122**, **145**, **147**, **150**, **155**, **157**, **159**, **167**, **173**, **178**, **184**, **210**, **228**

Estill Springs, **50**, **145**, **157**, **173**

F

Farris, **238**, **239**

Ford's Theater, **245**

Franklin, **18**, **44**, **50**, **51**, **55**, **61**, **65**, **66**, **68**, **69**, **70**, **73**, **74**, **78**, **86**, **89**, **94**, **123**, **128**, **138**, **159**,

182, **186**, **209**, **212**, **220**, **237**, **238**, **239**, **256**

Fremantle, **139**, **254**

French, **74**, **125**, **177**, **210**, **211**, **214**, **215**

French,, **125**, **177**, **211**, **214**, **220**, **224**

G

Garfield, **132**, **185**, **186**

General Joe Wheeler, **120**, **217**

General Joseph E. Johnston, **138**

General Leonidas Pope,, **139**

General Patrick Cleburne, **133**, **138**

General Thomas Crittenden, **143**

George Hawk, **200**

266

George Thomas, **122**

Gettysburg, **8, 9, 19, 63, 169, 170, 189, 191, 192, 240**

Goodman, **80, 90, 99, 185, 202, 204, 226, 227, 250**

Grant, **104, 191, 234, 240**

Grundy County, **1, 4, 7, 13, 17, 18, 19, 38, 48, 50, 55, 56, 57, 62, 64, 66, 68, 69, 70, 71, 76, 79, 80, 81, 82, 84, 87, 88, 89, 90, 92, 94, 95, 96, 98, 100, 115, 120, 122, 123, 124, 127, 128, 132, 140, 145, 166, 172, 175, 176, 178, 179, 180, 182, 185, 187, 191, 195, 197, 198, 201, 205, 207, 208, 209, 211, 216, 217, 218, 219, 220,** **226, 227, 230, 231, 238, 249, 250, 251, 253, 256, 258**

H

Hambright, **157**

Hampton, **200, 208, 209, 213**

Harris, **49, 50, 55, 56, 59, 83, 95, 106, 107, 108, 109, 110, 116, 124, 245, 261**

Henley, **226**

Hickory Creek, **70, 120**

Hill, **36, 79, 105, 211, 212, 213, 256**

Hillsboro, **62, 65, 68, 125, 145, 155, 164, 179, 181, 195, 211, 215, 238**

Hindman, **205**

Hoover's Gap, **144**

Hubbard's Cove, **57, 70,** **114, 117, 120, 125, 179, 183, 197, 251**

Hughes, **31, 217, 218, 223, 224**

I

Isaac Rust, **202**

J

J. C. Walker, **202**

James Winton, **90, 179**

Jasper, **51, 73, 80, 114, 197**

Jefferson Davis, **43, 45, 54, 101, 138, 140, 195**

Jepson, **221, 222, 223**

John Dibrell, **145**

John Hunt Morgan, **136**

Johnny Burnett, **197**

Johnston, **45, 47, 101, 105, 108, 139, 168, 195, 234, 235**

K

Kate Cummings, **168**

Kennesaw Mountain, **234**

Kitchell, **146**

Knight, **218**, **219**

L

Layne,, **91**, **97**, **209**

Lucy Virginia French, **124**, **125**, **176**, **177**, **210**, **211**, **212**, **220**, **224**

M

Manchester, **65**, **82**, **128**, **129**, **144**, **145**, **150**, **151**, **152**, **155**, **166**, **172**, **173**, **178**, **199**, **200**, **207**, **210**, **256**

Margaret Davidson Gwyn, **125**, **126**, **178**, **179**, **183**, **198**, **199**

Martha E. Swann, **196**

McMinnville, **19**, **72**, **75**, **79**, **80**, **81**, **113**, **114**, **119**, **125**, **136**, **143**, **145**, **164**, **165**, **173**, **174**, **179**, **212**, **223**, **256**, **257**

Memphis, **73**, **76**, **77**, **87**, **105**, **107**, **110**, **185**, **215**, **252**

Michael Gallagher, **184**

Murfreesboro, **65**, **116**, **130**, **132**, **133**, **136**, **142**, **143**, **207**

N

Nashville, **47**, **49**, **50**, **51**, **62**, **66**, **69**, **73**, **74**, **77**, **86**, **94**, **100**, **104**, **105**, **106**, **108**, **110**, **117**, **127**, **128**, **131**, **132**, **136**, **147**, **155**, **205**, **219**, **231**, **232**, **237**, **238**, **252**

Nathan Bedford Forrest, **104**, **105**, **116**, **136**, **156**, **212**, **233**, **238**, **240**, **255**

Northcut, **256**, **261**

Northcutt, **81**, **82**, **90**, **91**, **92**, **93**, **94**, **99**, **220**, **250**, **251**

P

Pelham, **13**, **18**, **57**, **62**, **64**, **66**, **68**, **69**, **70**, **73**, **83**, **86**, **89**, **91**, **95**, **99**, **113**, **114**, **115**, **118**, **119**, **122**, **145**, **146**, **149**, **150**, **152**, **153**, **155**, **157**, **158**, **159**, **160**, **162**, **164**, **165**, **167**, **172**, **173**, **174**, **175**, **178**, **180**, **184**, **185**, **191**, **197**, **201**, **203**, **207**, **208**, **209**, **211**, **216**, **226**, **232**, **239**, **252**

Phipps, **184**, **204**, **205**, **206**, **207**, **208**

Purdom, **211**, **212**, **213**, **220**

R

Robert E. Lee, **45**, **46**, **101**, **118**, **127**, **143**, **188**, **189**, **190**, **240**, **255**

Roberts, **65**, **263**, **264**

Rock Creek, **157**

Rosecrans, **132**, **136**, **138**, **143**, **144**, **145**, **154**, **158**, **162**, **166**, **169**, **170**, **178**, **185**, **231**, **233**

S

S. T. Witt, **202**

Savage Gulf, **71**, **218**

Sewanee, **78**, **79**, **86**, **87**, **140**, **145**, **232**

Shelbyville, **136**, **144**

Sherman, **106**, **131**, **234**, **235**, **236**, **237**

Solomon Goodman, **99**, **185**

Stone's River, **134**, **136**

T

Thomas, **11**, **12**, **63**, **80**, **85**, **87**, **90**, **98**, **109**, **117**, **118**, **121**, **126**, **143**, **158**, **167**, **168**, **172**, **199**, **200**, **202**, **203**, **233**, **237**, **238**, **247**, **255**, **261**, **262**, **263**, **264**

Tipton,, **91**, **120**, **262**

Tracy City, **64**, **75**, **85**, **87**, **92**, **114**, **149**, **164**, **165**, **179**, **184**, **185**, **186**, **203**, **204**, **215**, **220**, **221**, **222**, **223**, **231**, **232**

Tullahoma, **113**, **129**, **136**, **144**, **145**, **151**, **152**, **154**, **155**, **157**, **162**, **166**, **169**, **170**, **205**, **231**, **233**

U

Underground Railroad, **26**, **27**

Upson, **221**, **222**, **223**, **224**

V

Viola, **70**, **99**, **125**, **178**, **196**

W

Wagner, **201**, **203**, **215**

Wannamaker, **71**, **261**

Wesley Chapel Church, **183**, **184**

Wheeler, **120**, **136**, **151**, **158**, **206**, **209**, **217**, **218**, **232**

William E. Griswold, **180**

William Joseph Hardee, **141**

William Powell, **199**, **200**

William S. Whitman, **128**

Williams, **2**, **132**, **232**

Winchester, **50**, **51**, **113**, **114**, **123**, **139**, **147**, **157**, **158**, **162**, **164**, **165**, **175**

Made in the USA
Columbia, SC
11 June 2025